Jesus

The First 10,000 Days

How Jesus Came to Understand
His Identity, Calling, and Ultimate Destiny

Christopher Halls

O&U
Onwards & Upwards

Onwards and Upwards Publishers

3 Radfords Turf, Cranbrook, Exeter,
EX5 7DX, United Kingdom.
www.onwardsandupwards.org

Copyright © Christopher Halls 2019

The right of Christopher Halls to be identified as the author of this work has been asserted by the author in accordance with the Copyright, Designs and Patents Act 1988.

All rights reserved.

No part of this publication may be reproduced or transmitted in any form or by any means, electronic or mechanical, including photocopy, recording or any information storage and retrieval system, without permission in writing from the author or publisher.

Every attempt has been made to track down sources. Please notify the author if there are errors and omissions and these will be rectified.

First UK edition, published in the United Kingdom by Onwards and Upwards Publishers (2019).

ISBN: 978-1-78815-695-0
Typeface: Sabon LT
Graphic design: LM Graphic Design

Unless otherwise specified, scripture quotations are taken from THE HOLY BIBLE, NEW INTERNATIONAL VERSION®, NIV® Copyright © 1973, 1978, 1984, 2011 by Biblica, Inc.™ Used by permission. All rights reserved worldwide.

Scripture quotations marked (ESV) are from the ESV® Bible (The Holy Bible, English Standard Version®), copyright © 2001 by Crossway, a publishing ministry of Good News Publishers. Used by permission. All rights reserved.

Scripture quotations marked (KJV) are from The Authorized (King James) Version. Rights in the Authorized Version in the United Kingdom are vested in the Crown. Reproduced by permission of the Crown's patentee, Cambridge University Press.

Scripture quotations marked (The Message) are taken from THE MESSAGE. Copyright © by Eugene H. Peterson 1993, 1994, 1995, 1996, 2000, 2001, 2002. Used by permission of NavPress. All rights reserved. Represented by Tyndale House Publishers, Inc.

Endorsements

Who was Jesus of Nazareth? This question has been posed since the beginning of the Christian movement. Although we know a good deal more about Jesus than we do about Thales or Hillel, we want to know more and Chris Halls' book speaks to that longing. It sheds fresh light on the life and ministry of Jesus by calling attention to many unnoticed details in the narrative. It is not a kooky book – apparently, we have been given more information than we have realised. It is imaginative? Yes. Is it speculative? No.

Clark H. Pinnock[1]
Formerly Professor Emeritus of Systematic Theology,
McMaster Divinity College

When you consider that we only know about 10% of the life-story of the man whose birth, life, death, and resurrection has changed the history of this world and nations in it, it is unsurprising that much speculation and many genuine questions surround the rest of Jesus' life. How did he spend the first thirty years of his life? Was he naughty like other children? Who did he think he was? How did he come to the conclusion that he was the 'son of God'? And so on! Chris Halls, whom I have known for over twenty-five years, tackles these and many other questions about the early life of Jesus with consummate theological insight and literary skill, quoting the Bible, early church historians, Christian thinkers, and poets over the years, and gives us a penetrating insight into how Jesus thought about himself and how others have thought about his early life. This is a great read, which expands wonder and understanding, and I highly commend it.

Steve Thomas
International Team Leader, Salt & Light Ministries

---

[1] Clark Pinnock was commenting on a draft version the author discussed with him before his untimely death in 2010.

Often childhood and youth are described as someone's 'formative years'. Here Chris Halls brings together scholarship, faith, and imagination to offer a fascinating insight into the culture and scriptures that shaped the life of Jesus prior to his public ministry. This is a book for anyone who wants to understand and know Jesus better.

Nick McKinnel
Bishop of Plymouth

Chris Halls tackles a much-overlooked question, that of the growth of Jesus' self-understanding. For the contemporary Christian this is a vital aspect of engaging with the real humanity of Christ, and Chris Halls addresses it with care and lucidity as well as a patent love of the Scriptures. Warmly recommended.

Christopher Southgate
Professor of Christian Theodicy, Dept. of Theology and Religion, University of Exeter

If ever a book will make you think again, it's this one. "Oh no, not another gnostic account of Jesus' silent years, speculating on his early life," I thought initially, but this book is anything but 'gnostic'. It's not based on vivid imagination or doubtful texts, rather on what is 'hidden in plain sight' in scripture. Rooted firmly in the evidence of the four canonical Gospels, the author draws on Old Testament texts to illuminate the spiritual and historical context in which Jesus grew up. He shows us how Jesus fulfilled the Old Testament's prophecies; what, as a faithful Jew, he would have believed and practised; and how all this prepared him for the three years of ministry with which we are so familiar. As you see new things among old material, you will time and again find yourself saying, "I never knew that!" or, "That makes sense!" and find yourself, not just educated, but challenged about how you are living today.

Mike Beaumont
Taking Ground Apostolic Team, Salt and Light Ministries

To attempt to write about the so-called hidden years of the life of Jesus is both ingenious and quite challenging. The tendency toward speculation as well as artistic and creative licence have filled numerous works from the earliest centuries to the current day as authors have grappled to explore and reveal that which is concealed. Chris Halls manages to steer his way through these potential cul-de-sacs to provide the reader with a biblical, historical, and culturally informed work which provides a balanced and engaging [study], reflecting on the 10,000 days leading up to the beginning of Jesus' ministry. Drawing from a wide range of scholarship and spiritual writing over many centuries, the reader is led through various reflections and approaches which help to provide a lucid and highly satisfying work as he considers the identity, calling, and destiny of Jesus.

One of the great strengths of Halls' writing is in striking a balance of being informative and reflective as well as being devotional and spiritually engaging. New believers will therefore benefit from exploring what it would have been like for the human Jesus to grow up in his own cultural context; teachers and preachers will appreciate many of the links to history and the various comparative lists that inform good solid biblical study. All readers will find gems of understanding and delight as they consider the congruence found in the life of Jesus.

It is therefore a pleasure to commend this work to all who seek to understand Jesus through his human and spiritual development, thereby providing an authentic human example which may assist us in developing our own human and spiritual centre for expressing authentic discipleship and mission in the 21st century.

Dan Yarnell
National Co-ordinator, The Fellowship of Churches of Christ in Great Britain and Ireland; Senior Lecturer at ForMission College

A balanced and well researched book on the hidden years of Christ's life ... a solid Scriptural approach and ... very honest in separating truth and fiction.

Keith Gerner
Audio-Visual Ministries, N. Ireland

About the Author

 Christopher Halls has taught biblical studies on four continents in a variety of settings. He has served as a high school teacher and pastor in England, a theology lecturer in Nairobi, Kenya, and a principal of Christian schools in Canada. He is based in Exeter, Devon where he lectures in theology and has served as a chaplain at the University of Exeter.

To contact the author, please write to:

chrishalls@mac.com

More information about the author can be found
on the book's web page:

www.onwardsandupwards.org/jesus-the-first-10000-days

Join the Facebook group to keep up-to-date with book news:

www.facebook.com/groups/323646191544034

To friends at Isca Church, Exeter.

Acknowledgements

With special thanks to

Mike Beaumont, Peter Kay, and Mike Halls,
and my dear wife Jan,

for advice, support, and encouragement.

Contents

Foreword by Roger Forster

Jesus came home one day and asked, "Mum, what is a bastard? That's what they are calling me at school."

Mary looked up and said, "We don't use that kind of language in this house, my dear." She took up and rolled out the scroll of Isaiah until it reached chapter 7, verse 14. Then Mary said, "Before your father Joseph knew me... You know what I mean...?"

"Of course I do," Jesus replied.

Mary smiled and continued, "Well, God told me He was coming into the world of humans through just me, and it would mean you would be named Emmanuel – God with us."

"OK, thanks, Mum. What time's tea?" Jesus asked.

Even though that is speculative, at least something like this must have happened, if not exactly so. "Jesus kept increasing in wisdom and stature and in favour with God and men" *(Luke 2:52)*. Of course, Jesus could have had this knowledge by direct revelation from the Father to the Son when in prayer. We perhaps will never know. However, Jesus' realisation of his messianic calling and unique relationship to God the Father and things like this are better understood through meditating more in depth the circumstances, culture, and social and religious forces at work forming the boy and the man, Jesus.

That's why I love Chris Halls' book: *Jesus, The First 10,000 Days*. It's because I love Jesus and when you love someone, you want to know everything possible about him or her, and it usually takes a lifetime and a bit more to do it. This is not because Chris tells me fantasies as some apocryphal writings talk about these hidden years of Jesus. (One fantasy writing tells of Jesus as a boy making clay pigeons and their coming to life and flying away when He claps His hands.) Rather, because Chris provides the material for understanding a first century Jewish Orthodox boy and then man, and this enables me to understand Jesus better, with more depth and accuracy. Thank you, Chris, for this fine research; it will enable us to love Christ our Lord more fervently. I commend it to all, young and old Christians, to illuminate their imagination of Jesus, and that is where faith and love grow, leading in greater acts of the risen Christ.

Roger Forster
Founder of Ichthus Christian Fellowship, erstwhile Chairman of Evangelical Alliance, Vice President of Tearfund and author of 24 books

PREFACE

Lost? Secret? Hidden?

A mystery between two mysteries. A mystery apparently human between two mysteries divine. Jesus' hidden years.[2]

Robert Aron

He is arguably the most famous person who has ever lived, and yet words like "lost", "secret", and "hidden" are often used to describe the first 30 years of his life. Why do we know so little about Jesus before he began his ministry? We may wonder what he looked like? He has been painted and drawn more than anyone but are there any clues as to his appearance?[3] The four biographies we have – the Gospels in the New Testament – are avidly read by millions yet say so little about Jesus' early years. Is any knowledge of what happened in those years simply *lost* forever, or might we one day discover ancient manuscripts which satisfy our curiosity? Perhaps the details are intentionally kept *secret,* to be revealed only at the end of time. Or perhaps this information is simply *hidden,* awaiting discovery if we did but know where to look.

For many the desire to know more about Jesus has been insatiable. Through the centuries scores of books and articles have focused on aspects of his life and teaching and fascinating reconstructions of his life have been attempted – some incredibly speculative. The Hollywood film *The Young Messiah*[4] envisions what life might have been like for Jesus as a seven-year-old just beginning to understand his powers, as he and his family leave Egypt to return home to Nazareth. Based on Anne Rice's novel *Christ the Lord: Out of Egypt,* the film depicts Jesus in many ways as an ordinary child. He likes to run around and play, he is sometimes

[2] Robert Aron, *A Boy Named Jesus: How the Early Years Shaped his life,* xxi
[3] Joan E. Taylor provides some clues in her 2018 book, *What Did Jesus Look Like?*
[4] 2016, directed by Cyrus Nowrasteh; co-written by Betsy Giffen and Cyrus Nowrasteh

bullied, and he likes hearing Mary tell stories. But unfortunately, it seems the Bible is ignored and a strange embroidery of fragments from the so-called gnostic gospels is employed.[5]

The fictitious Jesus can also bring a dead bird back to life. He makes his sick uncle well and restores sight to a blind rabbi. As he travels from Egypt back to Nazareth with Mary and Joseph, the Jesus-character learns to hone his abilities and accept his identity and responsibility as the Son of God.[6] Vivid portrayals on film or in print may initially seem plausible but often owe more to the imagination than to historical realities.

Jesus: The First 10,000 Days attempts to steer clear of the excesses of the imagination (whether that of modern movies or early gnostic gospels) and journey closer to factual evidence. It is written from the conviction that much more can be known than is first apparent as we examine the signs and indicators within God's word with care and attention to detail, while keeping an open mind.

Early Christians wrestled with the nature of God as Trinity; it may not be a biblical term, nevertheless the Trinity is a thoroughly biblical concept – hidden in plain sight. In a similar way, might information about Jesus' early years also be there to discover, if we know where to look and are prepared to dig for treasure? The starting point for our quest will be the four Gospels, moving then to the rest of the New Testament. We will look into passages in the Old Testament that point to Jesus, and along the way will consider extra-biblical information from across a variety of disciplines available to the researcher.

Such an ambitious goal merits prayer; the following was first voiced by Augustine about his own work.

> O Lord, the one God, God the Trinity, whatsoever I have said
> in these books is of you, may those that are yours

---

[5] The gnostic gospels were written much later than the biblical accounts and are falsely attributed to the apostles (for example, *Gospel of Thomas*) and others in the New Testament (for example, *Gospel of Mary*). They are strange compilations of stories and sayings of Jesus and his followers which are without historical foundation and were rightly dismissed as heretical by the early church. For a helpful article on the gnostic gospels, see: *www.equip.org/article/the-gnostic-gospels-are-they-authentic/*

[6] Summary based on Roger Egbert's review: *www.rogerebert.com/reviews/the-young-messiah-2016*

acknowledge; whatsoever is of myself alone, would you and yours forgive.[7]

---

7   Edmund Hill (trans.), *The Works of Saint Augustine,* The Trinity, Prayer, 436

Jesus: The First 10,000 Days

CHAPTER ONE

Dawning of His Destiny

So much is observation. The rest is deduction.[8]

Sir Arthur Conan Doyle

If we consider things in their first growth and origin we will obtain the clearest view of them.[9]

Aristotle

Although Jesus is arguably the most influential person to have walked the earth, almost nothing about the first 30 years of his life is written about directly in the Bible. This is all the more remarkable when we consider that he died in his early thirties; some nine-tenths of his life, therefore, remain a mystery. The events surrounding his birth are well known and the last week of his life is recorded in great detail. The highlights of the three years before this are accorded a fair amount of space, but between his infancy and the start of his ministry, little is stated. Blaise Pascal, 17th century mathematician, philosopher, and theologian, wrote, "Of his 33 years he lived 30 without making himself known." Some might conclude that had it been important, we would have been informed. Or might it be that we have in fact been told more than is at first apparent?

In recent years scholars have vacillated between regarding the four Gospels in the New Testament as proclamations of faith, as focused biographies, or as distilled reports. Perhaps they are all of these; their purpose not to relate exhaustive detail but essential events from a particular perspective. Each Gospel writer presents a striking portrait of Jesus. To Matthew, for example, Jesus is someone steeped in the Law and traditions of Israel – the long-awaited fulfilment of Jewish expectation,

---

8   Sir Arthur Conan Doyle, *The Sign of Four*
9   Aristotle, *Politics,* Book 1

the Messiah.[10] To Mark, Jesus is the powerful leader who dramatically challenges the authority of Jewish leaders, and the spiritual powers causing sin sickness and death. Luke chronicles the life of Jesus as the heroic and compassionate Saviour who has come for all nations – not just the chosen people. Finally, in his unique poetic style, John reveals the powerful metaphors and rich visual imagery of Jesus' teaching, and his invitation for all to undergo spiritual rebirth.

However, of these four brilliant presentations, Mark and John tell us nothing of Jesus' earthly life before his ministry, and Matthew and Luke far less than most biographers would include. Only four of the 89 chapters in the Gospels tell us anything about the first 30 years of Jesus' life. Matthew and Luke each have two chapters and concentrate mainly on the events surrounding his birth and infancy. Apart from one incident when Jesus was 12, we are told no more about his childhood. Some have suggested that these chapters were added later after his death to satisfy the curiosity of his followers, yet there is no manuscript evidence for this. The 18 years passed over in silence are often referred to as the "hidden" years of Jesus.[11]

Other texts, not accepted by the first Christians as sufficiently trustworthy to be accepted into the New Testament canon, record events they claim occurred during the first 30 years of Christ's life, but these can hardly be trusted. Arising from different places around the Mediterranean between the second and eighth centuries, such documents are generally given short shrift by historians. Antonio Pinero's assessment is typical:

> These works are all far removed in time from the events they narrate. As a result, their authors are continuously carried off by fantasy and imagination ... Many times these sources contain information that is just impossible to harmonize; they are simply contradictory.[12]

---

[10] "Messiah" is the Hebrew term for the "Anointed One", or in Greek, "Christ".

[11] Four chapters narrate the events mostly surrounding his birth, 43 describe his three years of ministry, 29 his last week, 13 his last day.

[12] Antonio Pinero, *The Hidden Life of Jesus,* Preface. In fairness to Pinero's argument, he attempts some tentative conclusions about Jesus' life from these gnostic, apocryphal gospels which he believes can enrich or reshape our image of him. Others have been less restrained.

Our goal here is ambitious: to search for, in so far as is possible, that which is described so sparingly – the self-awareness of Jesus; to discern the process by which he came to conceive of his ministry and mission. To do this we need to weigh up evidence drawn from many disciplines. But Charles Carlston cautions:

> A series of approximations may give us substantial awareness of Jesus' self-understanding so far as this is deducible from the record, from the varied reflections of his words and actions in the surviving materials. Even this process, of course, is notoriously difficult.[13]

If this is the case, should we make the attempt at all? Yet the urge to discover more may lie in a desire to see in Jesus' own experience something that his followers might aspire to. Might a similar process to that experienced by Jesus in his enlightenment be the means by which we come to be aware of ours? Perhaps followers of Jesus can discern for themselves their own identity in God, what each of us has been called to, and even our ultimate purpose and destiny. By piecing together various strands of evidence from Jesus' experience, might clues be available to aid Christians on their journey of growth and discovery?

The primary source for this quest will be the biblical text. Since Jesus and his disciples had access to the same Spirit who inspired the "God-breathed" scriptures *(2 Timothy 3:16)*, it is not unreasonable to suppose there is a correspondence between his experiences and theirs. The Spirit who filled Jesus now filled their lives and interpreted truths revealed in the Hebrew scriptures about their identity, as well as his. Secondary sources – historical, social, political, and economic – can also be considered, and they form a colourful backdrop to provide us with a broader appreciation of Jesus' own experience.

Between the early childhood of Jesus (chronicled in the first two chapters of both *Matthew* and *Luke*) and his baptism as an adult are the "secret" years. Attempting to investigate this period of Jesus' life is fraught with challenges and church history is littered with examples of the fanciful and speculative, simply because we are no longer dealing with certainties, but with possibilities. How can we know what is truly factual? The premise adopted here is that everything must be weighed

---

[13] Charles Carlston, *Studying the Historical Jesus, Evaluations of the State of Current Research,* Prologue, 1

against the general revelation given us in the Old and New Testaments – and we are right to reject anything contrary to the letter or spirit of either.

This study is an attempt to retrace a spiritual journey, to sift historical and spiritual influences. But, as John Shelby Spong wrote, "Speculative re-creations of childhood and young adult adventures in the supposed 'lost years' in Jesus' life edify me not at all."[14] Fortunately, we have sufficient evidence to piece together significant aspects of relevant influences around Jesus as he grew to manhood. Some come from the Gospels and other books in the Bible, the edge pieces of a jigsaw puzzle, if you will, together with knowledge of Jewish traditions, and of the social, cultural, and political context in which Jesus grew up. By applying biblical principles to his life, a clearer picture begins to emerge.

Some may find the analysis too speculative in places; yet a disciplined use of the imagination is not harmful provided it keeps close to the text and does not make unjustified claims. Our goal is to see Jesus, the pioneer and perfecter of our faith *(Hebrews 12:2)* – how he blazed the trail for each of us, and how his life is an example and inspiration. Examining how he handled the patterns and pressures of everyday life can guide and help us in ours. As Jesus discovered his life's purpose, so we can press on to take hold of the reasons why Christ Jesus has taken hold of us *(Philippians 3:12)*; to be conformed to his likeness *(Romans 8:29)*. We are called to be imitators of Christ *(1 Corinthians 11:1; Ephesians 5:1)*; his example as a human being is the model for our lives *(Philippians 2:5)*. His experiences can help us in ours. How he received understanding and direction from the Father through the Spirit is the pattern for each of us. How he came to understand his identity and mission in life is through a process similar to the one we are to pursue.

Christmas has always been more popular than Easter – if church attendance is anything to go by. It is easier to celebrate the birth of a baby rather than the cruel death of a good man in his prime. Yet it was largely because of his death that the early church came to appreciate the uniqueness of the boy born in humble circumstances to a Jewish couple. Here was God in human form, they claimed; the incarnation of God's very being come to earth. Over the following centuries, scholars would describe his identity as that of the Son, the second person of the Trinity. Followers of Jesus today, in seeking to understand more of his

---

[14] From the Introduction to French historian Robert Aron's *A Boy Named Jesus,* i

distinctiveness, walk a tightrope; while acknowledging his deity, his humanity cannot be forgotten. We must bear in mind both earthly and heavenly factors as we come to the evidence.

Certain milestones in Christ's life were undoubtedly significant in his appreciation of his identity, calling, and destiny. But an exact timescale is, of course, beyond verification. Nevertheless, as we start to put together the pieces of the puzzle, a clearer understanding of Jesus' circumstances as a first century Jew, and inner spiritual life, begins to emerge. We know, for example, a good deal about the education of Jewish boys during this period from Hebrew sources.

A contemporary analogy may be helpful as we embark on our quest. Consider an athlete competing in the long jump. The athlete limbers up to keep his muscles warm. He makes his way to the line and mentally prepares himself for his turn. The track appears like a tunnel before him, his sights fix on the goal. He begins the run, accelerating, and all the while focusing on the board. Finally, he hurls himself into the air, every fibre stretched to extend his jump and squeeze out an extra centimetre...

Two things determine the success of an athlete – natural talent, and years of disciplined hard work. Every aspect of life comes under scrutiny in order to compete at the highest level. Before performing in front of the spectators, the athlete endures a rigorous training regime, and countless sacrifices are made. Preparation before the event is as crucial as physical and mental prowess on the day. The distance the athlete achieves is directly related to the timing, execution, and length of the run up. But this is scarcely noticed by onlookers for it is only the actual jump that is measured. This is all that counts. So it was for Christ. Thirty years of his life were spent in preparation – the "run-up", if you will. This receives scant attention in the Gospels – just four chapters. Nevertheless, what he achieved in the "jump" – the ground covered – is the focus of the rest of the New Testament and two thousand years of church history. This book is an attempt to look at the run-up, which was as remarkable as the jump itself, though in a different way.

Jesus, so we are told by Luke, began his ministry when he was about 30 years old *(Luke 3:23)*. The "run-up" had come to an end. From John's Gospel, we learn that Jesus' ministry lasted about three years – the jump itself.[15] Rounding the figures, we could say that Jesus spent 10,000 days living in obscurity far from the public gaze, with time enough to reflect on three fundamental issues:

- His identity: Who he was – Messiah
- His calling: What he was to say and do – Message
- His destiny: Why he had come to earth – Mission

These were followed by 1,000 days of sharing the good news – and of public scrutiny. The first 10,000 days of his life on earth were the run-up, the last 1,000 days the leap and landing. Those days hidden from the public eye were absolutely crucial to all he had come to achieve.

What follows then is an exploration of the dawning of Jesus' destiny – from his earliest moments of life, to his baptism 30 years later – by which time his sense of identity, calling, and destiny were fully formed. Our primary goal is to reconstruct, as far as the evidence allows, the first 10,000 days – the 'silent years' of Jesus' life – when this awareness and understanding was being formed. As we do so, we will draw inferences applicable to our own discipleship.

Yet, even before considering the 30 years of preparation before ministry, we must first attempt to delve into aspects of Jesus' incarnation when eternity stepped into time. With Anselm of Canterbury, we pray:

> I do not try Lord, to attain your lofty heights, because my understanding is in no way equal to it. But I do desire to understand your truth a little, that truth that my heart believes and loves. For I do not seek to understand so that I may believe; but I believe so that I may understand. For I believe this also, that unless I believe, I shall not understand.[16]

---

[15] The annual feast of the Passover is referred to in *John 2:13, 6:4, 11:55.* Another one is possibly alluded to in *5:1* – somewhere between 29-33AD. We are not far from the mark when we say it was about three years.

[16] Anselm, *Proslogion,* chapter 1, *www.stanselminstitute.org/files/AnselmProslogion.pdf*

CHAPTER TWO

Eternity Steps into Time

The Holy Spirit will come on you, and the power of the Most High will overshadow you. So the holy one to be born will be called the Son of God.

Luke 1:35

While gentle silence enveloped all things and night in its swift course was now half gone, your all-powerful Word leaped down from heaven, from the royal throne...

Wisdom of Solomon[17] 18:14-15

Our quest to understand the 'hidden years' of Jesus' life begins before his birth, to that moment when eternity stepped into time, when the "all-powerful Word leaped down from heaven." This is at the heart of the Christmas message when we celebrate God coming to earth in the flesh as a human being and living among us *(John 1:14; 1 John 4:2)*. We refer to this 'enfleshment' of God as the incarnation; a divinely ordained, decisive moment in history, "the fullness of time" *(Galatians 4:4)*, when the incomprehensible came to pass. German theologian, Erich Sauer notes:

> Leaving the free, unconditioned, world-ruling absoluteness of
> the divine form, the Son entered the limits of time and space
> of the creature.[18]

The One with the Father in the beginning, and through whom all things were made *(John 1:1-3)*, became microscopically small: a precious

---

[17] The *Wisdom of Solomon* was written in Greek around the time of Christ. It is to be found in the Apocrypha which, while not all Christians accept this as scripture, does provide us with insights into Jewish thinking at the time.

[18] Erich Sauer, *Triumph of the Crucified,* 13

treasure contained in an "earthen vessel" *(cf. 2 Corinthians 4:7)*. In a passage we will return to shortly, Paul describes how in doing so God set aside his "reputation" *(Philippians 2:7, KJV)* and submitted to the constraints of becoming a tiny embryo within Mary. The Son of God freely chose to be born as a human being, thus "emptying" himself as he set aside the privileges of deity, and being "poured out", by taking the form of a baby boy.

At the heart of our exploration is the supposition that at birth Jesus had no idea of his divine nature or the reason for his birth. If he really had become human we will need to explore if he had to assimilate information the same way you or I do. If he did, then from infancy he began a journey of self-discovery that would climax in the affirmation spoken over him at his baptism by which time he had a clear understanding of both his identity and purpose on earth. To trace the contours of this journey we start with the simplicity of the angelic announcement to Mary. Gabriel's words reveal the profoundest of truths and proclaim the unique and unprecedented partnership that was beginning between God and a humble Jewish woman *(Luke 1:26-38)*. A series of events was set in motion that would irrevocably change the history of humanity – even of the very cosmos *(Colossians 1:19-20)*.

The wonder and enormity of "our God contracted to a span, incomprehensibly made man"[19] still defies imagination. "Immensity cloistered in thy dear womb," penned the sixteenth-century poet John Donne.[20] How could the Maker of all things shrink so small as to become a single fertilised egg, barely visible to the naked eye? Then, to undergo cellular division and differentiation, specialization of tissues, and formation of organs, flow of blood, beat of heart, development of brain, spinal cord, and intricate nervous system, the everyday miracle of human growth in utero, experienced by God himself, deep within the womb of a Jewish peasant girl.

At the centre of the Christian message is the belief that Jesus Christ was fully divine, yet also fully human. He did not cease to be divine when he became a man, nor was his humanity partial or incomplete when he ascended to his Father after his life on earth. He was God in the form of man; as completely man as if he were not God; as completely God as if

---

[19] From Charles Wesley's hymn, *Let Earth and Heaven Combine*
[20] John Donne, *Annunciation* and *Nativity*

he were not man. He was neither a deified man, nor a humanised God. He was perfectly God and at the same time perfectly man.

How can we get our minds round this? How might an ant consider a human being in any meaningful way? The sight, sounds, the sheer size of a person would always overwhelm it and defy its comprehension. Were a man to try to communicate with an ant, so much would be beyond its grasp: love, beauty, truth, justice, mercy – not to mention a material world of laser surgery, 3D printing, space stations ... What parallels can we find for what God experienced in becoming human? C. S. Lewis' analogy is worth reflecting upon:

> Lying at your feet is your dog. Imagine for a moment, that your dog and every dog is in deep distress. Some of us love dogs very much. If it would help all the dogs in the world to become like men, would you be willing to become a dog? Would you put down your human nature, leave your loved ones, your job, hobbies, your art and literature and music, and choose instead of the intimate communion with your beloved, the poor substitute of looking into your beloved's face and wagging your tail, unable to smile or speak? Christ by becoming man limited the thing which to him was the most precious thing in the world; his unhampered, unhindered communion with the Father.[21]

God's strategy was to accommodate himself within the body of a human being who would faithfully bear his earthly and heavenly image and likeness *(Genesis 1:26; Colossians 1:15)* in order to represent perfectly who he is to humanity. Years later, whether quoting the words of an ancient Christian song, or perhaps his own *(Philippians 2:6-11)*, Paul reflects on how the second person of the Trinity experienced *kenosis,* a 'pouring out' of himself to become human.[22] Paul uses a phrase otherwise unattested in Greek to do so: "He emptied himself."

By choosing this term *kenosis* Paul emphasises that Christ did not selfishly exploit his own divine state of being, but by his own decision freely emptied himself of it, or laid it down, taking instead the form of a

---

[21] C. S. Lewis, from a radio address, quoted by I. D. Weatherhead, *A Plain Man Looks at the Cross*

[22] *Kenos* – originally meant "empty" (*keno-o* "to make empty"). Both adjective and verb were used in a literal concrete sense and figuratively.

servant by becoming man.[23] In one sense God "made himself nothing" *(Philippians 2:7)*, such was the enormity of the transformation he would experience.[24] Thomas Oord describes it as a "self-giving and others empowering love" which fits in well with the context of Philippians.[25]

In God all senses are perfect and infinite; he sees, senses, and is sensitive of all things. By "emptying himself", Christ denied himself and consented to the limitations of those he had made in his own image and likeness. Five senses must now suffice: like a world of vibrant colour reduced to a world of black and white or a three-dimensional world reduced to a plane; like a rich world of orchestral sound reduced to monotone. Heavenly reality was contained in an earthly image. Substance resembled shadow. The independent one became dependent. The 'man' became the 'ant'.[26]

The problem of how a limitless God could become limited in man can be illustrated by comparing two verses from Paul's letters:

For in him all the fullness of Deity dwells in bodily form.

Colossians 2:9; cf. 1:19

and,

Christ Jesus ... in the form of God, did not regard equality with God a thing to be grasped, but emptied himself.

Philippians 2:5-7

If, in the incarnation, all the fullness of God dwelt in Christ bodily, in what sense did he empty himself? Here we can only touch upon a topic that has exercised the minds of the greatest theologians. The dual nature of Christ and his relationship to the Trinity has been the subject of endless debate and the writing of countless volumes.

---

[23] See Kittel, *Theological Dictionary of the New Testament* III, 659 and Balz & Schneider, *Exegetical Dictionary of the New Testament* II, 282

[24] The nature of the *kenosis* Christ experienced is widely debated by believers today. For a contrary view to that expressed here, see Charles T. Buntin: *https://bible.org/article/empty-god*

[25] Thomas Oord, *The Uncontrolling Love of God,* 159

[26] "The eternal Son's divinity was not exorcised, but neither would it now be exercised. Having divested himself from divinity – economically though not ontologically – Jesus took to himself a fallen human nature – mortal and corruptible (Romans 8:3) and lived directed and dependent on the Spirit." Ponsonby, *God Inside Out,* 21

For nine long months, God, transitioned into the form – *morphe* (the same word in Greek) – of man. The self-awareness and understanding of one who lay in the bosom of the Father, in "closest relationship with the Father" *(John 1:18)*, was coming to earth to rest in the bosom of a humble peasant woman. But before this could happen he must first lay aside his divine attributes in preparation for birth. How was this possible?

Historian A. N. Wilson presents the view that the Christ-child was the Godhead veiled in flesh, and therefore that all knowledge and all power and all dominion were invested in that baby boy.

> As he lay in the manger, Jesus knew the entire future history of the world, until the moment when he would announce that it was time for the Last Judgment. He understood all the mysteries of creation. He understood, as no ancient scientist or mathematician could have done, the mysteries of astrophysics which are as yet unknown in the most advanced laboratories of the twentieth century. He has the capacity, merely by blinking an eyelid, to bring all creation to a stop, just as it was by the will of Jesus, true God and true Man, that creation had come into being in the first place.[27]

Yet this does not reflect what the New Testament actually says. If we are to take seriously Paul's description of Jesus 'emptying himself' at incarnation, it would seem that, as a baby and child, he would have been *unaware* of these things; that in order to become fully human[28] he gave up the attributes of God – omniscience, omnipotence, omnipresence, even consciousness of his eternal selfhood. His was a genuine sacrifice. As the apostle elsewhere expresses it, "though he was rich, yet for your sake he became poor" *(2 Corinthians 8:9)*. Here is true self-giving humility and self-denying impoverishment. It was a loss experienced too by Father and Spirit as their communion and love with the Son yielded a void of silence – at least for a season. By sending the beloved Christ they too embraced sacrifice and suffering.

Christ already possessed "equality with God", and neither abandoned that, nor regarded it as something "to be grasped". As Tom Wright points out:

---

27 A. N. Wilson, *Jesus,* 73
28 David Stern, *Jewish New Testament Commentary,* 597

> The proper translation of *ouch harpagmon hegesato* in Philippians 2:6 ... is "he did not regard his equality with God as something to exploit", something to take advantage of. In other words, he already possessed it, but did not regard it as an opportunity for self-aggrandizement after the fashion of pagan rulers.[29]

He humbled himself and chose to set aside the knowledge and power that was his by right. It was as if, for our sakes, God chose "divine amnesia", to become in one sense his own antithesis. At the moment of conception, he chose to move from omniscience to ignorance, a *kenosis* of knowledge, to a state of complete unknowing, an unparalleled self-abnegation.

Analogies can be woefully inadequate, yet it may be helpful to make a comparison using computer terminology. It was as if the Son of God's 'hard drive' was being erased completely, emptied, and wiped clean of all data. Only after his birth would it be restored, line by line, file by file, incrementally, over days, weeks, months, and years. At the same time the hard drive itself, which was his essential Deity, remained unsullied and intact.

As Keith Ward observes, the infinite God who is perfect goodness, condescends to...

> ...a limitation of infinity to encounter the finite on its own ground ... the infinite relates to us in a personal way, contracting infinity to finite form in order to bring us and all creatures capable of it to moral and intellectual maturity and lead our finite lives into fulfilling relationship with their infinite source and goal.[30]

From a place of total safety God was embracing a place of complete vulnerability. What more foolhardy thing could God have done! What courage must it have taken for an all-powerful God to risk descending to a planet known for its cruel violence, among those known for rejecting their prophets. He deliberately put himself where Satan and his demons could taunt and tempt him, and where lowly human beings could slap

---

[29] N. T. Wright, *Jesus' Self Understanding in The Incarnation,* 47-61
[30] Keith Ward, *God, a Guide for the Perplexed,* 233

his face and nail him to a cross.[31] Here is the courage of the Creator; a bravery that was displayed on Jesus' first night on earth and did not end until his last. He was risking all to enter a precarious and hostile environment; it was a *kenosis* too of security. The all-powerful was to become powerless. The one called the Word *(John 1:1)* became speechless. The communicator was silent. As popular Christian author Philip Yancey writes:

> The God who created matter, took shape within it, as an artist might become a spot on a painting or a playwright a character within his own play. God wrote a story, only using real characters, on the pages of real history.[32]

Perhaps he experienced a forgetting, a time when he was aware neither of the realm of heaven nor of earth. It would then have been a time of limbo, when he had no conscious communion with the Father. God laid aside his omniscience to become a *tabula rasa*, a clean slate, or as we might say, a blank canvas, upon which would be painstakingly painted stroke by stroke the knowledge a baby begins to assimilate from within the womb. But it was not simply information received through the physical senses, it was most importantly the heavenly intimations and impressions the Spirit would increasingly impress upon his own developing spirit.

How long would it be after his birth that Jesus would fully regain his self-awareness and fellowship with the Father and the Spirit? There may have remained with him a sense of the far country from which he had originally come. How often, we wonder, must Jesus have ached and yearned to be clothed with his "habitation which is from heaven, preferring to be away from the body and at home with the Lord?" – as the apostle Paul expressed it *(2 Corinthians 5:2-8)*. Sam Storm put it this way:

> The Word became flesh. God became human. The invisible became visible. The untouchable became touchable. Eternal life experienced temporal death. The transcendent one descended and drew near. The unlimited became limited. The infinite became finite. The immutable became mutable. The

---

[31] An idea developed by John Sanders in *The God Who Risks*, p.117 citing Philip Yancey's article, *Cosmic Conflict* (*Christianity Today* 38:14, 1994)

[32] Philip Yancey, *The Jesus I Never Knew*, 39

unbreakable became agile. Spirit became matter. Eternity entered time. The independent became dependent. The almighty became weak. The loved became the hated. The exalted was humbled. Glory was subjected to shame. Fame turned into obscurity. From inexpressible joy to tears of unimaginable grief. From a throne to a cross. From ruler to being ruled. From power to weakness.[33]

Are Christians sometimes at fault of emphasising Christ's deity at the expense of his humanity? In so doing we may fall into the error of teaching that Jesus only *appeared* to be human but was not really so *(1 John 4:2-3; 2 John 7).* This makes it harder to identify with Jesus as a real person – his humanity is denied us. As poet Steve Turner writes:

Like ...
Like your landlord becoming your lodger
Like your managing director up before you for an interview
Like Beethoven queuing up for a ticket at his own concert
Like a headmaster getting the cane
Like a good architect living in a slum built by a rival
Like Picasso painting by numbers
God lived among us[34]

We will explore this further as we look at the remarkable woman, his mother, Mary, and the earliest moments of her child's life.

---

[33] Sam Storms, *The Most Amazing Verse in the Bible, www.samstorms .com/all-articles/post/the-most-amazing-verse-in-the-bible.* Quoted in Andreas J. Kostenberger & Alexander E. Stewart, *The First Days of Jesus*
[34] Steve Turner, *Up to Date*

CHAPTER THREE

His Mother's Maker and His Mother's God

He was his mother's Maker and his mother's God. He formed the womb that gave him birth.

Joseph Parker

For nine months, he who is angels' Lord was hidden, love's furnace, in a little room, humbler than all, whom all adored.[35]

Tadg Gaelach O Suilleabhaim

The Virgin mother lulls to sleep, him who rules the cosmic deep.

Christmas Carol

If we probe beneath the familiar depictions of the Christmas story in Matthew and Luke, we glimpse heavenly realities that are often passed over. By bringing insights from physiology and psychology together with the biblical accounts, a fuller picture begins to emerge.

The divine DNA, or genotype of the Word, who "was with God in the beginning" *(John 1:1)*, was implanted into Mary's womb. "The power of the Most High will overshadow you" *(Luke 1:35)*. The infinitely complex life of God fused with the biochemistry of earth in order that God might become human. The Word left the Father's side and was conceived by the Holy Spirit within Mary; was "manifested in the flesh" *(1 Timothy 3:16)*. This is surely one of the profoundest mysteries of the universe – one of those secrets that belong to God alone *(Deuteronomy 29:29)*.

Jesus arrived in the tiniest, least-threatening form imaginable: a fertilised ovum; from which developed, as in every miracle of human growth, an embryo, a foetus, and finally a viable baby, bursting forth to join human beings on a speck of a planet in the midst of a vast universe.

---

[35] Tadg Gaelach O Suilleabhaim, *Pious Miscellany*

15

Through that segment of time, writes American author Max Lucado, a spectacular metamorphosis was taking place.

> While the creatures of earth walked unaware, Divinity arrived. Heaven opened herself and placed her most precious one in a human womb. God became a fetus. Holiness slept in a womb. The creator of life was created. God was given eyebrows, elbows, two kidneys, and a spleen. He stretched against the walls and floated in the amniotic fluids of his mother.[36]

Mary had, quite naturally, been confused, disturbed, and frightened by Gabriel's appearance to her *(Luke 1:29-30)*. But the words the angel then spoke may have perturbed her more; she would bear a child – before having any sexual relationship with Joseph, her husband-to-be. What would she have made of the angel's explanation that God's Holy Spirit would bring about the conception? She would have felt isolated, if she stayed in Nazareth – the object of suspicion and scandal. Hearing too from the angel that her relative Elizabeth was in her sixth month of pregnancy prompted Mary to spend the first three months of her pregnancy about 50 miles to the south of Nazareth in the hill country of Judea, with Elizabeth and Zechariah *(Luke 1:39,56)*. This was to be a significant time for her, in a place of security and reflection, where her faith could be nurtured and she could come to terms with the unprecedented responsibility she had been given – carrying the Son of God *(Luke 1:35)*. The journey south may have taken three days and was one she would repeat a few months later when she went with Joseph to Bethlehem for the census.

Five days after conception, a tiny bundle of cells – the most important cells in the universe – became embedded in the lining of her womb. By then she would have reached Elizabeth's home. Perhaps the words of one of the prophets came to mind as she thought about her child:

> Before I formed you in the womb I knew you, and before you were born I consecrated you; I have appointed you a prophet to the nations.
>
> *Jeremiah 1:5*

And yet she had been told her son would be more than a prophet – the holy offspring would be called the Son of God *(Luke 1:35)*. The

---

[36] Max Lucado, *God Came Near*, 25

Father knew the unique identity of Jeremiah, of Jesus, indeed, of each of us, before we were four or five days old – when implantation in the womb takes place.

Earlier, Elizabeth's husband had also experienced an angelic visit while serving in the Temple, preparing him for the birth of their son. Zechariah had found it hard to receive the divine message, since his wife had been barren for years and both of them were now old. As a result of his unbelief, he was then unable to speak for six months *(Luke 1:20)*, though could gesticulate to others what had happened *(Luke 1:22)*.

Through writing or mime, Zechariah informed his wife that she would give birth to a prophet who would turn many Israelites to God: "He will go on before the Lord, in the spirit and power of Elijah" *(Luke 1:16)*, and that this prophet would also be the forerunner to someone greater. He will precede the coming of the Lord, preparing a people for his arrival *(Luke 1:17)*.

After five months of quiet seclusion *(Luke 1:24)* Elizabeth intuitively knew upon Mary's arrival that it was this young woman, not herself, who was blessed above all other women by God. Her own child was the first to recognise the unborn Divinity, and "leaped in the womb" on hearing Mary's greeting *(Luke 1:41)*. Indeed, Elizabeth called Mary "the mother of my Lord". If Elizabeth's child was to be great in the eyes of the Lord *(Luke 1:15)*, Mary's would be greater – the Lord himself *(Luke 1:43)*. As she learned these things, Mary's natural anxieties and concerns would have given way to faith and hope. And as she shared with Zechariah and Elizabeth her experiences of the angelic visitation, their confidence and understanding would have grown too. The Lord was in control of their miraculous and extraordinary circumstances; he had caused both a barren woman and a virgin to conceive and nothing was impossible to him *(Luke 1:37)*.

It would be another two weeks before the embryonic Christ-child would develop a distinct heartbeat, and the foundations of brain, spinal cord, and nervous system would be laid. In five more weeks, just eight weeks after conception, a well-proportioned baby lay safe within Mary's uterus, little more than an inch in length and weighing 1/30oz, a mere gram. Soon every organ would be present and his heart beating sturdily; the stomach producing digestive juices, the bone marrow making blood cells; the kidneys beginning to function, even taste buds starting to develop. Indeed, most further changes from this point would be in size, weight, and increased efficiency of tissues and organ functions. Protected in the amniotic sac, the Son of God drank and swallowed, stretched, kicked, waved, and turned somersaults.

The first nine months of life are, in one sense, the most eventful, and major milestones are now well-documented. A baby's heartbeat can be detected eighteen days after conception. Just six weeks after conception signals from the foetal brain are evident. Dream patterns have been discovered around the eighth or ninth week. By about the tenth week the developing baby is capable of responding to touch and sound, and moving away from painful stimuli. Vocal cords are formed by the thirteenth week, and a baby at this stage is well able to recognise familiar sounds, such as his parents' voices.

Parallel to Jesus' physical development, the Spirit was at work forming his spirit – just as he does in every human being *(Zechariah 12:1)*. The breath of the Almighty was giving life *(Job 33:44)* and watching over his spirit *(Job 10:12)*. All the days ordained for [his development in the womb] were written in God's book before one of them came to be, as David described in *Psalm 139*. His words are also a prophetic picture of the process experienced by Jesus in becoming a human being. With the co-operation of the Spirit, the Father placed his hand upon the Son:

> You hem me in behind and before; and you lay your hand upon me, such knowledge is too wonderful for me ... You created my inmost being; you knit me together in my mother's womb ... my frame was not hidden from you when I was made in the secret place. When I was woven together in the depths of the earth, your eyes saw my unformed body.
>
> *Psalm 139:5-6,13,15-16*

David's song is Jesus' testimony. The Father saw the Son's unformed body, and in God's book "all the days ordained for me were written ... before one of them came to be" *(139:16)*. This is not so much a reference to what lay ahead for Jesus after his birth, as a recollection of all the days he had already spent in the womb.

Until a few decades ago, the thought that Mary's psychological state had any impact upon the child she carried might have been dismissed. But now, there is scientific evidence indicating that an unborn baby is affected by what goes on around him and his mother. At a physiological level, what a mother eats, drinks, or inhales passes through her bloodstream into her baby's body via the umbilical cord. It is now

18

understood that, since hormones are also able to reach the foetus through the mother's bloodstream, this undoubtedly influences the psychological state of the unborn child. Babies are also sensitive to a mother's behaviour; when she pats her stomach, talks, sings, or dances, the unborn child grows in awareness of her or his mother and her personality.

It seems that while a child in the womb is unlikely to be disturbed by each fleeting worry or concern of their mother, nevertheless, persistent patterns of negative emotions, such as chronic anxiety, anger, or stress, may well affect the baby. On the other hand, relaxed, positive feelings can infuse the baby with a sense of contentment, preparing them better for a balanced, happy, and serene disposition throughout life.[37]

If we concede that some kind of consciousness exists within days of conception then the first three months of a foetus' life are crucial. If emotions that grip the mother affect her unborn child too, then far from being cushioned from the outside world, the tiny baby feels the impact of these external factors. The womb was thus Jesus' first world. How he experienced it would have affected his personality and character predispositions. It was significant for Mary, and therefore for Jesus, that his first trimester was spent in an environment of faith and love, rather than fear and hostility.

Can we imagine what it was like for the Son of God, so recently transplanted from God's glory, the uniform of heaven, to toss and turn as a naked baby to the heartbeat of a young mother's being? Christian counsellor Joyce Huggett suggests that at times Mary's womb might have been an ominous home for Jesus.

> Jesus stepped straight from the spaciousness and perfection of Paradise into the desert-like darkness of a woman's womb. Having peeled off the privileges of deity, he squeezed himself into the limitations of our humanity. The Creator of mankind became a human embryo. The severity of this stripping spanned the womb and the tomb and re-shaped him physically and emotionally more than anyone before or since has been shaped.[38]

Joyce Huggett contemplates the bond that was being formed between Mary and her child:

---

[37] John Kelly & Thomas Verny, *The Secret Life of the Unborn Child*
[38] Joyce Huggett, *Formed by the Desert*

The result of this intimacy was a bonding between them that was both beautiful and unbreakable, even though their relationship was subject to a series of radical changes. The complete communion they enjoyed when Mary carried Jesus in her womb gave way to the partial communion of the pre-weaned infant and his mother. This phase, in turn, was resolved into the separateness every mother has to come to terms with when her baby becomes autonomous – still part of her, yet a little person in his own right.

The Father had ordained that his Son would pass the first trimester of his life on earth in the security and loving environment of a righteous family who would be able to reassure, comfort, and instruct Mary about God's dealings with her. Elizabeth and Zechariah had much to discover and think through for themselves – but they had nearly six months head-start on Mary in processing their own situation. They had time to come to terms with the miracle that had happened to them, and to direct Mary's thoughts about the greater miracle that was occurring inside her.

Shortly after Elizabeth's child, John, was born, Mary returned to Nazareth. By now her own child would be entering the third stage of development in the womb, tissues and organs maturing and movements intensifying, despite the increasingly confined space around him. It was now only a matter of weeks before the final stage – birth, and entry into the human race. He was ready; was the world?

CHAPTER FOUR

Emptied Himself of All but Love

Welcome, all wonders in one sight!
Eternity shut in a span!
Summer in Winter, Day in Night!
Heaven in earth, and God in man!
Great little One! Whose all-embracing birth
Lifts earth to Heaven, stoops Heaven to Earth.[39]

Richard Crashaw

Though Christ pre-existed in the form of God, yet he did not look upon equality with God as a prize which must not slip from his grasp, but he emptied himself, divested himself of the glories and prerogatives of deity.

Philippians 2:5-7 (Lightfoot's translation)

The path of the righteous is like the first gleam of dawn, shining ever brighter till the full light of day.

Proverbs 4:18

The heart of God is one of love. Charles Wesley, founder of Methodism in the eighteenth century, expressed this powerfully in one of his well-known hymns:

He left his Father's throne above,
    so free so infinite his grace!
Emptied himself of all but love,
    and bled for Adam's helpless race.[40]

Love is the one quality it is impossible for God to "empty himself" of; for to do so would be to deny his very essence, the core of his being *(1 John 4:7-21)*. There can be no stronger demonstration of this love, as

---

[39] Richard Crashaw, *The Shepherd's Hymn*
[40] Charles Wesley, *And Can It Be?*

Wesley clearly saw, than Christ's death on the cross. His self-giving love, demonstrated so powerfully at the crucifixion, becomes the interpretative lens through which we see every other facet of God's nature and aspect of Christ's life.[41]

The *self-emptying* of God finds its complete and most conclusive fulfilment at Calvary, yet at the same time there never was a *fuller* revelation of his essential being: "All (God's) fullness, *pleroma*[42], dwells in Christ in bodily form" *(Colossians 1:19)*. Behold the man who is at once both 'empty' yet 'full'. In defending Christ's deity, some appear to diminish his humanity while others defend his humanity at the expense of his deity. Through the centuries, theologians have tried – like tightrope walkers – to balance the truth of Jesus' divinity and humanity. It is clear that whatever else Jesus set aside in coming to earth, the fullness of his *persona*, his essential loving nature, and sense of justice, holiness and righteousness, were all undiminished.

When Jesus was born he knew nothing of his unique identity nor of what his life would hold. In this respect, he was no different from any other child coming into the world. Yet, from the first gasp of this baby's first breath, a turning point in history was taking place; a child, seemingly like any other born in Israel at the time, was the one who would perfectly reveal God to man. Before he could do this though, Jesus had much to learn. He had first to be instructed in his true identity and destiny as Son of God.

For this to occur, a heavenly and earthly dynamic partnership formed. From the vantage point of heaven, the Father and the Spirit were to oversee and orchestrate what the child Jesus experienced and how he would interpret this. From an earthly perspective, Joseph and Mary, far less aware of the importance and consequences of the project, were to parent Jesus with the loving care of those who had caught a glimpse, but not a complete revelation, of the significance of their task. Heaven and earth were united in a mission of salvation; a synergy hitherto unparalleled in human experience.

"Who has known the mind of the Lord?" challenged the prophet, *(Isaiah 40:13f, cf. Romans 11:34)*. How would Jesus come to know the

---

[41] Greg Boyd, *Crucifixion of the Warrior God,* see Vol. I. chapter 4, 141ff. Boyd quotes Moltmann approvingly, "The crucified Christ … is the key for all the divine secrets of Christian Theology."

[42] *Pleroma* – that which fills, hence: completeness, abundance

mind of the Lord? Nothing could be more important. The enormity of the project entailed the greatest of risks. How would the child respond to the Spirit's promptings and the Father's instruction? Would he receive or reject them? Submit or rebel? Would Joseph and Mary be equal to their task? Would they be able to process and assimilate all they had learned about their Son in a way that empowered them to communicate this? Would they be able to lead Jesus beyond the limits of their own understanding and knowledge? And would he choose to accept these insights or to ignore them?

The process of receiving revelation from God is described by Paul when writing to the Corinthians. It can help us understand this from Jesus' perspective *(1 Corinthians 2:9-16)*. What Jesus had not seen with his eyes nor heard with his ears, nor had conceived in his mind, everything in fact that the Father had prepared for the Son he loved, was revealed to him through the Holy Spirit *(cf. vs.9-10)*. Only the Spirit could do this, because he sought out the heart of the Father's plans and intentions and communicated these to Jesus' spirit within him. Deep calling to deep.

Jesus would have to live, not from a perspective based on his natural senses alone, but from the vantage point of the Spirit who had been given to him by God. All this was so that Jesus could clearly understand what God had freely given him. This would enable him to discern, and later to express publicly, spiritual truths in spiritual words. In adulthood, as a spiritual man he evaluated and processed all things. He had come to know the mind of the Lord as the Spirit instructed him.

> The Spirit searches all things, even the deep things of God. For who knows a person's thoughts except their own spirit within them? In the same way, no one knows the thoughts of God except the Spirit of God. What we have received is not the spirit of the world, but the Spirit who is from God, so that we may understand what God has freely given us.
>
> *1 Corinthians 2:10-12*

For the child Jesus to be taught, the Father and the Spirit must also teach Joseph and Mary; a process that might well have begun before their child was born – perhaps even in their own childhood years. Those stewarding the upbringing of Jesus needed first to know God and his ways. As faithful Jews, the parents of both Mary and Joseph must surely have laid up a rich spiritual heritage their children could draw upon. In the school of prayer and of the Word, Joseph and Mary would have come to understand and trust in the goodness and love of God and his purposes for his people, Israel. Their stewardship of truth would become central to what they passed on to their Son. Their love and fear of the Lord would inform the manner of their instruction.

We can imagine that in the years prior to Jesus' birth, Father and Spirit had orchestrated to divinely inspire this ordinary couple's parenting of Jesus. Never had such a project been embarked upon before. Their privilege – and their burden – was not merely to inform a child that he was known and loved by God and had plans to fulfil like a prophet of old, such as Jeremiah *(Jeremiah 1:4-10)*, but that he was the pre-existent Son of God. His was a mission to perfectly reveal God to the world and be its Saviour.

In the sixteenth century, French protestant reformer John Calvin pointed out that unless we wish to deny that Christ was made a real man, we must not be ashamed to confess that he voluntarily submitted to all those things which cannot be separated from human nature.[43] A thousand years earlier, Leo the Great, the controversial fifth century Pope, had written something similar:

> He assumed "the form of a servant" without the defilement of sin, enriching what was human, not impairing what was divine: because that "emptying of himself," whereby the invisible made himself visible, and the Creator and Lord of all things willed to be one among mortals, was a stooping down in compassion, not a failure of power. Accordingly, the same who, remaining in the form of God, made man, was made man in the form of a servant. For each of the natures retains its proper character without defect; and as the form of God does not take away the form of a servant, so the form of a servant does not impair the form of God.[44]

I have suggested that the newborn Jesus did not come with an adult understanding of who he was – that he was not omniscient as a baby, God "gift-wrapped" as a child with the knowledge of the Creator. Rather, that it would be more accurate to consider the infant Jesus with the body, soul, and spirit of a child; in physical bodily form with a human

---

[43] Quoted in Robert Aron, *A Boy Named Jesus*, xx
[44] Pope Leo, *The Tome of Leo*

mind and human nature, and therefore with all the limitations this implies.

Probing deeper, some have speculated that God incarnate had two distinct minds or systems of mentality. Philosopher Thomas Morris argues for what may be called the "eternal mind of God the Son", with a distinctively divine consciousness encompassing the full scope of omniscience, empowered by the resources of omnipotence, and present in power and knowledge throughout the entirety of creation. In addition, he argues that Jesus also had a distinctly earthly mind with a consciousness that developed from conception and birth, and throughout his time of growth into maturity.

In Morris's view, Jesus' human mind drew visual imagery from what he saw around him, and concepts from the languages he learned. His earthly mind with its range of consciousness and self-consciousness was therefore thoroughly human, Jewish, and first-century in nature.[45] By living out of his human body and mind, he took on the form of our existence and shared in the plight of our condition. In *Our Idea of God*, Morris continues:

> The human mind was contained by, but did not itself contain, the divine mind ... Everything present to the human mind of Christ was thereby present to the divine mind as well, but not vice versa. There was immediate, direct access from the human mind to the divine mind, but no such converse immediacy of access. In so far as Christ normally chose to live his earthly life out of his human resources alone, the words he spoke and the actions he performed by means of the body were words and actions arising out of his human mind. He had all the mental, intellectual, emotional and volitional resources we all have, lacking none. And it was these, not his divine resources, that he typically drew on for the personal history he enacted on this earth.[46]

But are we really to believe that Jesus had "two minds"? New Testament scholar Daniel Wallace arrives at a different conclusion in his

---

[45] Tim Bayne, *The Inclusion Model of the Incarnation: Problems and Prospects. Religious Studies,* Vol 37:2, 125-141

[46] Thomas Morris, *Our Idea of God: An Introduction to Philosophical Theology*

discussion of this issue.[47] Perhaps we should distinguish between the eternal qualities that belong to God alone and those that relate to a person's character:

> We need to think of the divine attributes in two categories: moral attributes and amoral attributes. The moral attributes are those attributes that speak of God's morality – justice, mercy, love, goodness, kindness ... The amoral attributes are those that speak of God's sovereignty – omniscience, omnipresence, omnipotence, infinity, eternity ... What is interesting to observe in the Gospels is that a clear line of demarcation can be seen with reference to Jesus: he never fails to function on the level of the moral attributes, but frequently does not display the amoral attributes. In other words, the moral attributes seem to be hard-wired to his human consciousness, while the amoral attributes seem to be subject to the guidance of the Holy Spirit and come to the human conscious level at the Spirit's choosing. At the same time, since he does occasionally demonstrate the amoral attributes, there is no denying his deity. Although Jesus Christ has both a human and divine nature, he is not two persons. He has one consciousness. It is not enough to say that his divine nature does not always operate at the level of his human consciousness. Why? Because it is only the amoral attributes that fit this description.[48]

The New Testament presents us with a portrait of the mind of Jesus – extraordinarily wise and discerning, but less than omniscient. For all his character strengths, in coming to earth Jesus limited his internal powers, depending instead to turn heavenward for resources, just as we too must do. We observe someone who not only shared the joy and anguish of the human condition but was also influenced by a first-century Jewish world view to a considerable extent. A truthful picture of the

---

[47] Wallace distinguishes what he describes the moral and the amoral attributes of God which can be misleading as we tend to equate 'amoral' with 'immoral' which is far from what he means.

[48] Daniel Wallace, *When Did Jesus Know? The Translation of Aorist and Perfect Participles for Verbs of Perception in the Gospels,* Bible.org, 2004, *https://bible.org/article/when-did-jesus-know-translation-aorist-and-perfect-participles-verbs-perception-gospels*

incarnation must account for this. An understanding that Jesus freely renounced, even if only temporarily, part of his unrestricted divinity can satisfy this requirement. In this he did not act of his own will alone but with the agreement and cooperation of the Father and the Spirit.

Let us consider further the attributes of omnipresence and omnipotence. God became 'localised' in Jesus; one person, restricted to being in one place, at one time. Nevertheless, he promised that after his departure from the earth he would be with his disciples until the end of the age *(Matthew 28:20)*. Through the promised *Paraclete*, the Holy Spirit, Jesus would be enabled to be with all disciples, in all places, and at all times *(John 14:26, 15:26, 16:13)*.

What of omnipotence? Was the man Jesus all powerful? Nothing in the Gospels suggests that before the Holy Spirit came upon him at his baptism Jesus had greater powers than other people. Stories of miracles performed by the boy Jesus appear in various apocryphal gospels, but these can be discounted in the light of *John 2:11*, where we read that the turning of water into wine was the first of Jesus' miraculous signs – not one in a series that had begun in his childhood. Only after his anointing with the Spirit did Jesus begin his demonstration of God's power over nature, death, sickness, and evil (see *Mark 5-6*).

Did Jesus then become omnipotent once he had received the Spirit? It would seem not, as we read, for example, that "he could do no miracles there, except he laid his hands on a few sick people and healed them". It may have been people's unbelief preventing them from bringing their sick to Jesus in Nazareth (see *Mark 6:5-6*), although this seems unlikely in view of his reputation at the time. Jesus might have chosen to limit himself because of their lack of faith and trust, or there may be other undisclosed reasons why he did not have the power in this instance.

Jesus undoubtedly had access to enormous power, for we read that the Father would not deny him twelve legions of angels – 72,000 – with which to defend himself should he choose *(Matthew 26:53)*. (Since one angel was deemed sufficient to destroy Jerusalem *[1 Chronicles 21:15]* or an army *[Isaiah 37:36]*, twelve legions would have been more than enough to overthrow the Roman Empire.) Yet, Jesus, like his disciples after him, had to receive the power of the Holy Spirit before he became a 'worker of miracles' *(Acts 10:38, cf. Acts 1:8)*; then he could exercise the gifts of the Spirit, including those of faith, healing, miraculous powers *(1 Corinthians 12:28,9-10)*. It seems therefore, that though mighty powers were available to him, Jesus, like all humanity, needed to walk in humble obedience and accept only that which was within the Father's will for him in terms of supernatural works *(John 5:19-20)*.

Jesus chose to live as one under authority, like the centurion he commended *(Matthew 8:8-10)*. He submitted to the Father and to the self-imposed restrictions on his knowledge, his presence, and the exercise of his power. Such boundaries were set before his incarnation when Jesus chose to lay aside privileges that were his by divine right, in order to live in the world as a human being. Jesus decided to relinquish the security of heaven and become subject to a fallen environment where sin, death, and decay are the rule. He came "in the likeness of sinful flesh" *(Romans 8:3)*.

As John Stott comments:

> The Son came neither "in the likeness of flesh", only seeming to be human, as the Docetists taught, for his humanity was real; nor 'in sinful flesh', assuming a fallen nature, for his humanity was sinless, but 'in the likeness of sinful flesh', because his humanity was both real and sinless simultaneously.[49]

By becoming man, Jesus chose neither to cling to the worship that was his by right, nor God's glory – the *Shekinah*, that clothed him in splendour, nor the knowledge and power that was his from eternity. The Gospels reveal what this meant practically in his interactions with others.

When Jesus was a man, we read of him being amazed or surprised; "on hearing this, Jesus was surprised" *(Matthew 8:10)*; "he was amazed at their unbelief" *(Mark 6:6)*; "Jesus was surprised when he heard this" *(Luke 7:9)*. His was an emotional response to learning something new. At other times, we read of Jesus growing in knowledge: "Jesus, knowing that they intended to come and make him king by force, withdrew again to a mountain by himself" *(John 6:15)*.[50] If Jesus learned, then it follows that he was not omniscient as a man.

We also read of him sometimes asking questions. Was this intentional in order to elicit a response from his listeners, or because he actually did not know certain things? For example:

[49] John Stott, *The Message of Romans, The Bible Speaks Today*
[50] See also *Matthew 12:15,25, 16:8, 22:18, 26:10; Mark 8:17, 12:15; Luke 9:47; John 6:61, 19*

At once Jesus realized that power had gone out from him. He turned around in the crowd and asked, "Who touched my clothes?"

Mark 5:30

"How many loaves do you have?" he asked. "Go and see." When they found out, they said, "Five and two fish."

Mark 6:38

Jesus asked the boy's father, "How long has he been like this?" "From childhood," he answered.

Mark 9:21

After three days, they found him in the Temple courts, sitting among the teachers, listening to them and asking them questions.

Luke 2:46

Ignorance does not signify failure, fault, or necessarily weakness. Jesus declared that he was ignorant of the "day or hour" of his return *(Mark 13:32)*; but significantly this statement was preceded by an astonishing claim for the infallibility of his teaching: "Heaven and earth will pass away, but my words will never pass away" *(Mark 13:31)*. This distinction between ignorance and intentional fault is crucial. It is impossible to think of Jesus as mistaken about his fundamental convictions, or deliberately teaching the erroneous views of his age as truth, if we hold to the idea that he is the one who died to save us from the penalty of sin *(Mark 10:45)*.

The New Testament is clear that Jesus never sinned, yet we surely wouldn't be wrong to think that Jesus might have made mistakes growing up as a child. Unintentional errors are a vital part of learning. The toddler stumbles before he walks; the child needs correcting before realising a better way to achieve something. It takes practice to form letters correctly on a page – it doesn't happen perfectly the first time. Did Jesus, for instance, perfectly form the letters of the alphabet the first time he tried writing? Could he count to ten after hearing the numbers spoken only once to him? Did he use a hammer and a saw as skilfully as he did after years in the carpenter's workshop? Surely not. The Gospels maintain a balance between Jesus' unique and growing awareness of the Father and his will *(Luke 2:49)* alongside his growth in knowledge and understanding *(Luke 2:46)*.

If our faith grows and matures, would this not also have been the case for Jesus? Richard Kropf writes about the different stages of faith he might have undergone. After describing the instinctive faith of infancy, he writes of the intuitive faith of childhood nurtured in the context of a loving family:

> Jesus' sense of compassion, his love for nature, his love of children, his childlike sense of freedom to ignore social conventions – all these speak of an atmosphere that was trustful and warmly supportive of a childhood that was rightly summed up in Luke 2:40. "Meanwhile, the child grew to maturity. He was full of wisdom and God's favor was with him."[51]

Jesus grew in wisdom as a child *(Luke 2:52)* and even as an adult did not know everything exhaustively. As we have seen, this implies that when he came to earth Jesus experienced some sort of self-limitation in his absolute knowledge of both the past and present. If he were omniscient, he could not grow in knowledge since he would always know all things. Jesus expressed surprise at the faith of the centurion *(Matthew 8:10)*, grief at the unbelief of Jerusalem *(Luke 19:41)*, sorrow at the death of Lazarus *(John 11:33-35)*. His emotional responses were to real events rather than a pretence or an act to impress bystanders. The verb used in each case is one that is regularly used of others being surprised or amazed. In every instance, the connotation seems to be an emotional reaction that accompanies learning something new.

It was therefore a deliberate decision by the Trinity that the incarnate Son would know only what man could know through life experience and the indwelling Spirit. "He had to be made like his brothers in all respects" *(Hebrews 2:17)*. A logical part of that emptying would be to empty himself of his self-awareness.

Throughout eternity the Spirit had always been his constant companion. But at the incarnation the Spirit assumed a new role. From the moment of Jesus' conception, the Spirit became his guardian and mentor as well. From previously knowing all things, Jesus chose to know only what a son of Adam could know. Cyril of Alexandria declares, "He

---

[51] Richard W. Kropf, *The Faith of Jesus – the Jesus of History and the Stages of Faith,* 17

complied with the laws of the nature which he had made his own."[52] The fullness Jesus possessed was a clear and unsullied conduit for the presence and will of God to be expressed.

Like each of us, Jesus was a unique individual experiencing human needs – tiredness *(John 4:6)*, hunger *(Matthew 4:2)*, thirst; and emotions – sorrow, anger, joy. Yet we also read of Jesus' knowledge as greater than that of his contemporaries. He sometimes knew people's thoughts through ways not experienced by ordinary people *(Matthew 12:25)* or knew things that could not be learned by mere observation *(John 13:1,3)*.

Some passages speak eloquently of Jesus' supernatural knowledge – a knowledge that defies any natural explanation. For example, in *Matthew 17:27* Jesus knew that the first fish Peter would catch would have a *stater*, a large coin, in its mouth, enough to pay the Temple tax for both Peter and Jesus. In *John 1:48* Jesus declared to Nathaniel that he saw him when he was under the fig tree and that because of this he knew him to be a man without guile.

Although Jesus had knowledge of the human and spiritual realms beyond that of ordinary people, this can partly be explained in terms of supernatural insights, "words of knowledge" he received from the Spirit *(1 Corinthians 12:8)*. In clothing himself with "the body that had been prepared for him" *(Hebrews 10:5)*, he relinquished the ability to be everywhere at once and to know everything at once. We should see Jesus on earth as neither omnipresent, omniscient, or omnipotent – by God's choice and active will, not by accident or incidentally. As American theologian John Walvoord states:

> Christ restricted the benefits of his attributes as they pertained to his walk on earth and voluntarily chose not to use his powers to lift himself above ordinary human limitations.[53]

Augustine vividly describes the paradox before us:

> Maker of the sun, he is made under the sun. In the Father he remains, from his mother he goes forth. Creator of heaven and earth, he was born on earth under heaven. Unspeakably wise, he is wisely speechless ... He is both great in the nature of God, and small in the form of a servant...

---

[52] Robert Aron, *A Boy Named Jesus*, xx
[53] John F. Walvoord, *Jesus Christ our Lord*

Man's Maker was made man that he, Ruler of the stars, might nurse at his mother's breast; that the Bread might hunger, the Fountain thirst, the Light sleep, the Way be tired on its journey; that the Truth might be accused by false witnesses, the Teacher be beaten with whips, the Foundation be suspended on wood; that Strength might grow weak; the Healer might be wounded; that Life might die.

Augustine of Hippo

We have arrived at the edge of the deepest mystery:

- As man, Jesus was born of Mary *(Luke 2:7)*; as God, he was in the beginning *(John 1:1)*.
- As man, he grew up *(Luke 2:52)*; as God, he does not change *(Hebrews 13:8)*.
- As man, he slept in a boat while a storm raged *(Matthew 8:24)*; as God, he upholds the universe by his power *(Colossians 1:17; Hebrews 1:3)*.
- As man, he died *(Luke 23:46)*; as God, he is eternal life *(1 John 5:11-12,20)*.

Scientists attempt to understand the nature of light. Theologians try to understand the Light of the world *(John 8:12)*, and God – the source for all the laws of physics. Both scientist and theologian face a similar dilemma with an apparent incompatibility – an antinomy – between two apparent truths. Each is true on its own, but it is hard to see how they can be true together; side-by-side, they seem irreconcilable, yet both are undeniable. For the physicist, there is experimental evidence to show that light behaves like waves, and equally that it behaves like particles. It is not apparent how light can be both waves and particles, but the scientific evidence is there. For the theologian, there is evidence to show that Jesus was fully human, and equally that he was fully divine. Two seemingly incompatible positions must be held together and both must be treated as true. Such a necessity scandalises tidy minds, but there is no other way if we are to be loyal to the evidence.

CHAPTER FIVE

Abba, My Father

To be one with the infinite in the midst of the finite and to be eternal in the moment.[54]

Friedrich Schleiermacher

The perception of an infinity which lies beyond yet in and through all things, in the face of which we are speechless, before which our lives shiver into nothingness, and yet in whose light we see eternal significance transfiguring the world.[55]

Keith Ward

Luke was clearly fascinated by the circumstances surrounding Jesus' birth. The first two chapters of his Gospel are part of his "careful investigation" *(Luke 1:3)* as he introduces significant individuals who shaped Joseph and Mary's understanding of who this child was and would become. Firstly, there was Mary's extraordinary dialogue with the angel *(1:26-38)*; then, her visit with Elizabeth *(1:39-56)*. Hearing the experiences of Zechariah and Elizabeth, and the circumstances of John's miraculous conception, would have greatly influenced Mary's awareness – months before her child was born *(1:5-25,57-80)*. After Jesus' birth, both parents' understanding deepened as they gleaned more from the shepherds' visit *(2:8-20)*, from Simeon's words in the Temple *(2:25-35)* and those of the prophetess Anna *(2:36-38)*.

Luke allows us to glimpse how profoundly these encounters affected Jesus' parents. For example, when the shepherds visited the newborn Jesus with their tales of angels, of God's glory, and voices from heaven, Luke records how "Mary treasured up all these things and pondered them in her heart" *(2:19)*. A month or so later, after Simeon had

---

[54] Schleiermacher, *Speeches on Religion,* Speech 2, 1799
[55] Keith Ward, *God, a Guide for the Perplexed,* 30

prophesied over Jesus, Joseph and Mary "marveled at what was said about him" *(2:33)*. Recalling another visit to the Temple twelve years later, Luke recounts, "But his mother treasured up all these things in her heart" *(2:51)*. That Luke catalogues their responses to these incidents when writing his Gospel perhaps 60 or so years afterwards, is testimony to their lasting influence. The messages they had received, the words spoken over their child – all these were indelibly etched upon their consciousness and could not be taken lightly; they were to be pondered, treasured, discussed, and prayed over, and were surely discussed often in the coming years by Joseph and Mary and other trusted family members.[56]

As he grew, Jesus' family clearly played a special role in confirming to him what he was already beginning to sense in his spirit. But first they too had to come to understand the heart of the Good News; that God had become a human being in Jesus. What trust God placed in Mary and Joseph as 'foster' parents; an ordinary man and woman entrusted to fulfil an awesome task.

Psychologically speaking, it is unlikely that anyone could have been such an outgoing and compassionate a person as Jesus, had he been deprived of motherly nurture and love. If the common Near-Eastern pattern of mother-child relationship, still evident today in the Arab world, where it is often customary for male children to be nursed until age three or four (although girls are usually weaned earlier), is any indication of what was then the norm, we must conclude that Jesus' infancy was outstandingly supportive for a future life of faith.[57]

Few marriages in the Bible can withstand close scrutiny, yet that of Joseph to Mary appears exemplary. We can infer that from Jesus' earliest moments he was a child bathed in the prayer and love of his godly parents who took seriously the responsibility of prophetic insights they had been privileged to receive. Just 40 days after her baby's birth, Mary heard words from Simeon that would prepare her for her own pain, "a sword will pierce through your own soul" *(Luke 2:35)*. As parents, they carried a heavy sense of responsibility and must have relied on the prompting of

---

[56] Acts 1:14 records that Mary is with the other disciples before Pentecost, and there is the real possibility that Luke met her and asked her to describe her experiences. How would he have known these circumstances otherwise?

[57] Richard W. Kropf, *The Faith of Jesus – the Jesus of History and the Stages of Faith,* 15

the Holy Spirit for comfort and wisdom. How could they otherwise know when and what they should say to their child concerning his mission that he would "save his people from their sins" *(Matthew 1:21)*, or be "a light to bring revelation to the Gentiles and the glory of your people Israel" *(Luke 2:32)*?

How did Mary and Joseph feel at the time of these experiences? Were there moments of astonished silence, of fearful awe, and of ecstatic rapture? Were they caught up in a sense of the holy, simultaneously puzzled, amazed, and overwhelmed? Were these miraculous insights, like the intoxication of beauty, almost too intense to bear? As stewards of the words of God and angels, the sayings of wise men and simple shepherds, and stories from relatives and strangers, so much rested on their good parenting. A holy fear and reverence must have been at work in their lives. Their understanding would be formative in nurturing Jesus' self-awareness; their insights a channel of revelation into their child's own development.

Yet, feeling inadequate to communicate such depths of reality to their son, they would in fact have been perfectly positioned to do so, living as they were in humble reverence and the fear of the Lord. Through the richness of their God-encounters, they were therefore well-qualified for the challenging task of informing and instructing their son in matters of the mind, heart, and spirit.

How soon after their return from enforced exile in Egypt to Nazareth did they begin to talk to Jesus of his destiny? As loving parents, sensitive not to overburden their young child with a weight of truth too onerous for his years, they must have waited for inspiration about what they shared. Both Mary and Joseph would have had knowledge of Israel's history and prophecies passed down from one generation to the next. Would they direct his attention to Isaiah's Suffering Servant prophecies, or David's messianic psalms? Whatever significant part Mary and Joseph undoubtedly played, God clearly did not intend to leave it all to them alone. Jesus was the only person since Adam never to have an earthly father. (Paul describes him as "the heavenly man" and "the second man is from heaven" [see *1 Corinthians 15:47-49*].) However righteous and good Joseph was *(Matthew 1:19)*, he was inadequate to teach Jesus all he needed to prepare him for his life's work. He could train him well in natural things, but the uniqueness of Jesus' ministry on earth required divine parenting.

Let us take a step back to the unique event of incarnation; Father, Son, and Holy Spirit each actively participated in the moment of Christ's divine conception. Their involvement was then equally crucial during the first 30 years of Jesus' life. Together the Godhead worked in harmony to prepare his understanding and character for what lay ahead. In order for *Immanuel*, Jesus, to be *God with us*, Father and Spirit had first to be immanent to Jesus *(Isaiah 7:14)*. We may look on this Father-Son relationship as referring essentially to closeness, dependency, reliability, openness, confidence, and love. Paul characterises the eternal relationship between the persons of the Trinity in terms of grace, love, and fellowship *(2 Corinthians 13:14)*. The Father protected and provided, disciplined, trained, and educated the Son. This role of the Fatherhood of God was crucial to Jesus' development, as we will see more closely in a later chapter.

For 30 years the Father and Spirit in partnership trained the Son. By the time Jesus began speaking publicly he knew perfectly the will of his Father *(Matthew 7:21, 12:50; John 7:40)* and the mind of the Spirit *(Romans 8:27)*. In referring to Father and Son, we acknowledge the unique character of their relationship with one another that began with the incarnation. But did this wonderful new event – incarnation – mark a new phase of their relationship? Previously, David had referred to these two persons of the Trinity as Yahweh and Adonai (*Psalm 110:1:* "The LORD said to my Lord"). Now it seems God was doing something new: Yahweh is now the Father, Adonai is now the Son.

One of the most fundamental qualities of Jesus was his humility. His entire life was one of submission to the Father and dependence upon his will: "The words I say to you I do not speak on my own authority, but the Father who dwells in me does his works" *(John 14:10)*. The Son could do nothing by himself *(John 5:19)*.[58] The humility displayed in the incarnation would characterise Jesus' entire earthly life – from childhood to crucifixion.

Hindsight is helpful in providing insights into the early life of Jesus. Setting information from his public ministry alongside other New Testament passages describing events involving his early followers, we can extrapolate what Jesus' own experiences might have been. To illustrate this, we can probe a little deeper into an early experience of Jesus – his encounter as a twelve-year-old with priests in the Temple

---

[58] *cf. 5:30,41, 6:38, 7:16,28, 8:28,42,50, 14:24*

(Luke 2:41-51). It is not unreasonable to think that Mary and Joseph reflected on this incident, especially since there seemed to be a mild rebuke in Jesus' reply to them and he seemed to be expecting them to have understood better. And again, it does not seem unreasonable to think that they would have looked back over the years to see how they had come to understand things now more clearly.

In Aramaic, Hebrew and other Middle Eastern languages, *Abba* was used by adults and children alike. 'My father' best conveys the spirit of the meaning.[59] The vernacular of Jesus' day – his everyday language – was Aramaic. Although written in Greek, the New Testament occasionally preserves the original Aramaic that Jesus spoke. In *Mark 14:35-36* we read,

> [Jesus] fell to the ground and prayed that if possible the hour might pass from him. "Abba, Father," he said, "everything is possible for you. Take this cup from me. Yet not what I will, but what you will."

Not only would *Abba* have been, in all probability, the first word Jesus uttered, it was also his first recorded word: he had to be about *Abba*'s business[60] *(Luke 2:49).* The same word was used by the Father at Jesus' baptism, to remind him of his Sonship *(Matthew 3:17).* He used it too in Gethsemane when he prayed for us *(Matthew 26:39,42).* And it was the last word on his lips as he died for us – "Father, into your hands I commit my spirit" *(Luke 23:46)* – probably because the terminology impacted the early church so much.

In *Matthew 11:20-24* we read that Jesus rebuked the cities who were rejecting his message. After this there seems to be a change of focus for the text then literally goes on to say, "At that time Jesus answered and said..." Whom was he answering? Jesus then suddenly broke into prayer.

---

[59] Geza Vermes, in *Jesus and the World of Judaism* decries the "improbability and incongruousness of the theory" that *Abba* means "Daddy" and that "there seems to be no linguistic support for it", p.42. He holds that *abba* can either be understood as "the father" or the more personal "*my* father". For an interesting article about the meaning and use of *Abba*: *https://www.thegospelcoalition.org/article/factchecker-does-abba-mean-daddy*

[60] We should note in passing that Luke and Matthew use the Greek for father, *pater,* rather than the Aramaic, *abba,* although there may not be any significance in this.

> "I praise you, Father, Lord of heaven and earth because you have hidden these things from the wise and learned and revealed them to little children. Yes, Father, for this is what you were pleased to do."
>
> *Matthew 11:25-26*

It seems that while aware of those around him, Jesus was even more aware of his Father's presence. He continued, "All things have been handed over to me by my Father; and no one knows the Son except the Father; nor does anyone know the Father except the Son *(Matthew 11:27)*. Jeremias the New Testament scholar interprets this verse like this:

> Like a father who personally devotes himself to explaining the letters of the Torah to his son, like a father who initiates a son into the well-preserved secrets of his craft, so God has transmitted to me the revelation of himself, and therefore I alone can pass on to others the real knowledge of God.[61]

On another occasion Jesus said, "The Son ... can do only what he sees his Father doing ... the Father loves the Son and shows him all he does" *(John 5:19-20)*. Had Jesus' awareness of his Father's presence, rather than suddenly occurring at the start of his public ministry, been developing throughout his childhood and into manhood? Before he encouraged his disciples to say, "Our Father," had Jesus been addressing God as *Abba* – his heavenly Father? Did he intend for his own experience to be mirrored in his followers' lives?

19th century theologians seeking to discover the irreducible content of Jesus' message settled on two concepts they regarded as non-negotiables. They recognised that he spoke continually about the Fatherhood of God and of his kingdom – the 'rule of God'. Little wonder then that his most famous teaching, the Sermon on the Mount *(Matthew 5-7)*, is peppered with references both to God as Father *(Matthew 5:48, 6:3,6,8,9,14...)* and (in many of Jesus' parables) to his Father's kingdom (for example, *Matthew 13*).

In the Old Testament, Israel is described as God's Son (for example, *Hosea 11:1*), but it was virtually without parallel at the time of Jesus for an individual to address God in such a personal term as *"Abba"*; this would have been considered presumptuous and disrespectful. Yet Paul

---

[61] Jeremias, *The Prayers of Jesus*, p.51

follows his Lord's example, twice describing the believer's relationship to God with this word. Where could Paul have got this from, other than Jesus?

Because you are his sons, God sent the Spirit of his Son into our hearts, the Spirit who calls out, "Abba, Father." So, you are no longer a slave but God's child; and since you are his child, God has made you also an heir *(Galatians 4:6-7)*.

Similarly, in his letter to Christ-followers in Rome he writes:

> The Spirit you received brought about your adoption to sonship. And by him we cry, "Abba, Father." The Spirit himself testifies to our spirits that we are God's children.
>
> *Romans 8:15-16*

The Roman practice of adoption guaranteed to the children the same rights and privileges as for natural children. Yet here Paul is describing something more intimate and personal than just our legal status. For it is the Holy Spirit who assured Jesus of his identity as Son of the Father who now confirms that the same is true for each of us as sons and daughters. As the Spirit's presence gave Jesus confidence in prayer as God's beloved Son, so he can do the same today for every child of God.

CHAPTER SIX

When I Was a Child

Adam prefigured him, heaven held him, earth grasped for him, creation groaned for him, the creature travailed for him, humanity cried for him, Israel foretold him, Joseph dreamed of him, the archangel announced him, John preceded him, the archangel heralded him – but Mary bore him. Blessed art thou among women! [62]

John Metcalfe

Josef ben-Iacob, carpenter, Miriam bath-Ioachim, his wife, Yeshua, firstborn son

(as their names might have appeared in the census records)

David the psalmist's words have extra poignancy when we recall how Jesus uttered the opening line of *Psalm 22,* "My God, my God, why have you forsaken me," as he hung on the cross. Many scholars think that the whole song was in Jesus' thinking and this would include these phrases:

You brought me out of the womb; you made me trust in you even at my mother's breast. From birth I was cast upon you; from my mother's womb you have been my God.

Psalm 22:9,10

From his first breath till his last, Jesus trusted in God. The Father and Spirit certainly watched over this child – a new creation – continually affirming Jesus' identity and amplifying his understanding. The Spirit perhaps even made intercession for him with groans that words cannot express – as he would later for all his followers (see *Romans 8:26*).

Isaiah had prophesied of Jesus' heritage, and described the activity of the Holy Spirit in his life: "A shoot will spring from the stem of Jesse ... The Spirit of the Lord will rest on him" *(Isaiah 11:1-2)*. As a tiny shoot,

---

[62] John Metcalfe, *The Birth of Jesus Christ*

the fragile, delicate, sprouting of new life, Jesus must surely have perceived the gentle presence of the Spirit resting on his consciousness. As a growing baby distinguishes sights and sounds, so Jesus' spirit, sensitised by the Holy Spirit, would have discerned the things of God around him. Isaiah sets before us words that apply to every stage of Jesus' earthly pilgrimage: "He will delight in the fear of the Lord, and he will not judge by what his eyes see, nor make a decision by what his ears hear" *(11:3)*. (Later we examine some of Isaiah's insights into the Messiah and see how these scriptures influenced Jesus as he read them for himself.)

The Holy Spirit would have begun to witness to his spirit that he was the child of God and from this he began to develop an unshakeable confidence of his unique relationship to the Father *(cf. Romans 8:15-16)*.

Jesus was born into a culture richly permeated with signposts to the reality of God's presence in everyday life. Mary gave birth to a son and Joseph called his name Jesus *(Matthew 1:25)*. From the lips of Jesus as a child and as an infant, God ordained praise *(cf. Psalm 8:2)*. In countless ways, God paved the way for Jesus' entry into the world through revelations of his will and his word. One such was a message spoken through an angel:

> You are to give him the name Jesus because he will save his people from their sins.
>
> *Matthew 1:21*

Joseph and Mary were told separately by God that they would have a boy and that he should be called *Yeshua*, Jesus *(Matthew 1:21, Luke 1:31)*; a name with a wealth of Old Testament connotations, conveying inspired leadership, miracle-working power, and spokesmen with remarkable prophetic insights.

Joshua (Hebrew: *Yeshua*, from *Yehoshu'a*, meaning *Yahweh is salvation*) recalls the anointed leader who brought Israel into the Promised Land. Joshua (the anglicised version of *Yeshua*) succeeded Moses as leader of the Israelites and led the conquest of Canaan.[63] In

---

[63] Interestingly, Joshua's original name was Hosea – a variant of *Hoshe'a*, which also means 'Salvation' *(Numbers 13:16)*. Two other Old Testament prophets had names with similar meaning: the miracle worker Elisha (from *Elishu'a*, meaning 'My God is salvation') and the great prophet Isaiah (from *Yesha'yahu*, meaning 'Yahweh is salvation').

Joseph and Mary's day, this was the fifth most popular name of the time, indeed, four of 28 High Priests in Jesus' time were called *Yeshua*, perhaps because it carried powerful historical significance.[64] *Yeshua*. What other name could have been so special yet so familiar? *Myriam* (rather than our anglicised Mary)[65] was the most common name among women at that time, and *Yosef* (Joseph) was second most common for men after *Shimon*. Their names would appear as ordinary as Mr and Mrs Smith seem to us today.

Bethlehem, *Bet Leim* ('House of Bread'), so called as it was in the 'breadbasket' for the nation, was a small settlement six miles south of Jerusalem. In the Old Testament we read of the town's association with Rachel, Ruth, Jesse, and most importantly David, Israel's greatest ruler; a Bethlehemite shepherd who was anointed king here *(1 Samuel 16:1-13)*. How fitting that the one "born king of the Jews" *(Matthew 2:1)* and called by the angel "Son of David" *(Luke 1:32)* should start his life on earth here. As had been prophesied long before:

> You, Bethlehem Ephrathah, though you are small among the clans of Judah, out of you will come for me one who will rule over Israel, whose origins are of old, from ancient times.

> *Micah 5:2*

The significance of Jesus' name and birthplace would not have been lost on his parents. Both were at once very normal and commonplace and yet at the same time special and unique.

The shortest verse in the Bible tells us that the man Jesus wept at the tomb of his friend Lazarus *(John 11:35)*. But as a baby, did he cry? Not if we are to believe that favourite children's carol *Away in a Manger*: "The little Lord Jesus, no crying he makes." But, yes, if we agree with the

---

[64] In contrast to the early biblical period when a great variety of personal names were in use, there were relatively few names among the Jewish population of Israel in the first century. The name *Yeshua* was one of the most common male names, tied with Eleazar for fifth place behind *Shimon, Yosef, Yehudah* and *Yohanan*. In a survey of the literary and epigraphical sources of Jesus' day, Hachlili found that nearly one out of every ten males known from the period was named Jesus. See Rachel Hachlili, *Names and Nicknames of Jews in Second Temple Times, Eretz-Israel* 17 (1984): 188-211.

[65] "Mary was named after Moses' sister, Miriam; and Elizabeth in remembrance of Elisheva, the wife of Moses' brother, Aaron." Charlotte Allen, *The Human Christ: The Search for the Historical Jesus,* 36

writer of *Once in Royal David's City*, "Tears and smiles like us he knew." The theology of traditional songs may be based more on sentiment than scripture, yet the question and its answer are relevant if we are to accept the humanity and vulnerability of Jesus in a hostile world. As Irenæus, one of the early church fathers, wrote:

> ...the Word of God, our Lord Jesus Christ, who did, through his transcendent love, become what we are, that he might bring us to be even what he is himself?[66]

Most certainly the newborn Jesus cried. Surely this was one of the first signs of his humanity. He was nursed and fed like any baby, circumcised on the eighth day as a Jewish son, carried like any child; helped to walk and taught to speak. If this were not so, the Gospel writer's words would make little sense: "Jesus grew in wisdom and stature" *(Luke 2:52)*. If he already had these attributes fully, then there is no point in mentioning that he increased in them. Was the infant Jesus fully aware of who he was? Did he look with bemused eyes at all the adults around him as he played the part of a child? Was he fully capable of speaking but simply refrained for appearance's sake, as the Quran and Muslims claim? If these things were true, it would mean that Jesus' human experience was but a sham.

When Jesus, at 40 days old, was presented in the Temple at Jerusalem, Mary and Joseph offered the prescribed sacrifice for a poor family *(Luke 2:24)*; a pair of turtledoves or two young pigeons were all they could afford *(Leviticus 12:8)*. While the gift of the Magi *(Matthew 2:11)* would perhaps later have provided for the family's needs for their time as refugees in Egypt, it is doubtful whether they ever ceased to be anything other than a poor family. Joseph had to provide for his household; economic conditions were hard and the level of taxation high. Jesus would have lived, therefore, like most ordinary people, in a one or two-room, two-level dwelling where the living area was raised slightly above the stalls for the animals.

The small houses were gathered close together to share limited resources. Houses were often joined together with a shared inner courtyard where a few animals could be kept. The proximity of the homes and close family ties led to a spirit of neighbourliness. Water was not readily available and needed to be brought in daily; bathing was only

---

[66] Irenæus, *Against Heresies, (Adv. Hear. V, Pref.)*

common during the rainy season. The outer walls were plain and the flat roofs, where people socialised and where in the hot season they slept at night to catch the cool night-time breeze, were made of tile or mud. Inside, there was little furniture: mats provided bedding and, in the middle of a mud floor, a small charcoal fire heated the home during cold weather.

The faith of the family would also have been reflected in their clothes. The child Jesus would have worn clothing prescribed by the Law. From the age of three he would have had a coat bearing the *sisit*, or fringe, described in *Deuteronomy 22:12*. He may also have worn the *tephillin* (phylacteries, *Deuteronomy 6:8*), small boxes bound to arm and head containing the scriptural verses: *Exodus 13:1-16; Deuteronomy 6:4-9, 11:13-21*.

Life in first century Galilee and the village of Nazareth was simple. At home Jesus' family would have had two meals each day; bread was the main food. The light brunch – often flat bread, olives, and cheese (from goats or sheep) – was carried to work and eaten at mid-morning. Evening dinners were more substantial, consisting of vegetable (lentil) stew, bread (made from barley for the poor, wheat for the rich), fruit, eggs, and sometimes cheese again. In Galilee fish was also common with one of the meals; but red meat was reserved for special occasions such as festivals and banquets. Locusts were a delicacy. Olive oil was used for cooking, and honey was the main sweetener.[67]

In *Acts 10:14* Peter declared that he had never eaten anything "profane and unclean". Since he was one of Jesus' closest disciples for three years, we may conclude that Jesus too observed *Kashrut*, the dietary laws, and from childhood had eaten only kosher food. (Unlike the Pharisees, ordinary Jews did not adhere to all the meticulous regulations of *Kashrut* which had become more complicated by the first century.) Jesus would have said a blessing before and after meals, not to 'bless' the food, but in praise and thanks to the Creator *(Deuteronomy 8:10 cf. Matthew 6:41, 26:26)*. The traditional blessing is: *Barukh attah 'Adonai 'elohenu Melekh ha-olam ha-motsi lechem meen ha-arets* – Blessed are you, our Lord God, King of the Ages/Universe, who brings forth bread from the earth.

---

[67] See Alfred Edersheim, *The Life & Times of Jesus the Messiah* for further details about Galilee.

"Having entered upon life as the divine infant, he began it as the human child, subject to all its conditions, yet perfect in them," taught the Jewish scholar Alfred Edersheim.[68] As a child, Jesus would have looked like a typical Jewish boy with identifiable features – though nothing out of the ordinary *(Isaiah 53:2)*. He would have picked up a Galilean accent (the same accent that would give Peter away as a northerner in Jerusalem many years later, *Mark 14:70*) and the rich traditions of his Jewish culture.

He [Jesus] grew up before him [the Father] like a tender shoot,
like a root out of dry ground.

Isaiah 53:2

To adapt Paul's exhortation to believers at Philippi: Jesus was blameless and harmless, a child of God without fault in the midst of a crooked and perverse generation among whom he would shine as the light of the world *(Philippians 2:15)*; a sign of hope and promise in a barren world.

Mary and Elizabeth must have shared a special bond of friendship; and it is not hard to imagine the mothers talking with their sons about the miraculous events surrounding the conception and birth of each. As we shall see, it is likely that Jesus and John knew each other from early childhood, and we can perhaps imagine some of their conversations together. Did Jesus offer encouragement and direction to John? Was the clarity of John's prophetic calling derived from insights Jesus offered him? His first recorded words about Jesus were, "Here is the Lamb of God who takes away the sin of the world" *(John 1:29)*. Had the Father given this revelation directly to John, or might it first have come from Jesus? How frequently over those 10,000 days might they have interacted, discussed the future, and prayed together? Of course, if we are to be true to the biblical text, such discussions, however tempting, lie beyond our remit – a point the gnostic gospels consistently failed to realise.

As Mary and Joseph meditated on the words of the angel, perhaps, like Matthew, they looked at the passage in Isaiah about the promised Immanuel, 'God with us' *(Isaiah 7:14)*. Did they appreciate that he would possess the land *(Isaiah 8:8)*, thwart all opponents *(Isaiah 8:10)*, and

---

[68] Alfred Edersheim, *The Life & Times of Jesus the Messiah,* chapter 9, *The Child-Life in Nazareth*

45

appear in Galilee of the Gentiles as a great light to those in the land of the shadow of death (*Isaiah 9:1-2*, quoted in *Matthew 4:13-16*)? Did they understand that their son would be called "Wonderful Counselor, Mighty God, Everlasting Father, Prince of Peace", whose government and peace would never end as he reigns on David's throne forever *(Isaiah 9:6-7)*?

> The results of the hidden years of Jesus' childhood are seen in his adulthood, and the completion of Mary's task is seen in what he achieved. He changed the face of the world, and she was the instrument that made this possible. We have in him no magic wonder-boy or man bypassing human exigencies. He hungered, thirsted, cried, needed comforting, and, in the quality of his mother's response, he discovered the means to answer hunger, thirst, and suffering in the lives of others. Jesus found in his mother what he needed – and she did not let him down.[69]

Jesus was not the only child of Joseph and Mary. *Mark 6:3* and *Matthew 13:55-56* indicate that he was the eldest of at least seven, possibly eight or more, children – though some Christian traditions, eager to maintain the idea of Mary's perpetual virginity, interpret these as cousins.[70] Their names indicate a strong commitment to Israel's traditions: James *(Jacob)*, Joseph *(Joses)*, Simeon *(Shimon)*, and Judas *(Judah)*. The comment, "Aren't all his sisters with us?" indicates that he had at least two sisters – perhaps more.[71] From the genealogy that opens Matthew's Gospel we learn that Jacob was the father of Joseph the husband of Mary, the mother of Jesus *(Matthew 1:16)*. It is clear that

---

[69] Jack Dominian, *One Like Us: A Psychological Interpretation of Jesus,* 70

[70] Family members are specifically mentioned in *John 2:12; Mark 3:31-35, 6:3; John 7:3-9; Acts 1:14; Galatians 1:19; 1 Corinthians 9:5.* (This last reference suggests that more than one of Jesus' brothers became a follower; and that at least two married brothers took their wives with them on mission trips.)

[71] Jesus' family tree is explored in more detail in chapter 13, *Fisherman, Prophet, and Messiah.* For a thorough analysis, see Richard Bauckham, *Jude and the Relatives of Jesus in the Early Church.* See also his article *Relatives of Jesus* in Ralph P. Martin and Peter H. Davids, eds., *Dictionary of the Later New Testament and its Developments:* 1004-1006. *https://katachriston.wordpress.com/2011/06/07/richard-j-bauckham-on-the-relatives-of-jesus/*

Joseph was proud of his Jewish patriarchal heritage and named his own first son in memory of the child's grandfather as well as the great patriarch Jacob, in Genesis. Brother Joseph was of course named after his father and also another patriarch. Judas and Simon were given names of Jewish Maccabean war heroes.

Did the siblings play, shout, run, and tumble like all children? Why wouldn't they? As the oldest and therefore typically carrying more responsibility than the younger ones, Jesus must have learned pastoral skills from an early age. Did he sort out squabbles, tend to grazed knees, comfort a sick toddler, and sing a baby to sleep? Probably. After all, that's what most big brothers do. Did he learn the craft of his carpenter-father, watching the shavings fall on the dusty workshop floor, as skilful hands deftly carved and created practical furniture for the villagers? Almost certainly, since that's what every Jewish boy did – learn his father's trade from an early age. In many ways Jesus' childhood was no different from that of other children. As a young child, he would have spent time with friends playing games similar to hopscotch and jacks. Archaeologists have found whistles, rattles, toy animals on wheels, hoops, and spinning tops in Israel. Perhaps Jesus played with such toys. Older children and even adults found time to play too, usually it seems with board games; a form of draughts was popular.

But did Jesus, the holy child *(Luke 1:35)*, sin, stray from God's ways and the holy law? Not according to his own testimony *(John 8:29; 15:10)*, nor that of New Testament writers: Paul *(2 Corinthians 5:21)*, Peter *(1 Peter 2:22)*, and John *(1 John 3:5)*. Several times we read that Jesus had a human nature like ours *(Hebrews 2:11,14,16,17; Romans 1:3)*. He took on the nature of Adam but did not yield to its inherent weaknesses. Although "tempted in every way, just as we are" *(Hebrews 4:15)*, he did not respond self-indulgently to any temptation. As a young child, an adolescent, and a teenager, he learned to depend upon the power of his Father and the presence of the Spirit, fully surrendered to God's will. To observe each stage of Jesus' life must have been as refreshing as it was challenging.

But this picture of close family connections does not mean they were initially all supportive. We need to consider statements that Jesus' family did not believe in him *(John 7:3-5).*[72] Even his mother did not wholly understand him and was perhaps embarrassed by her son's strange behaviour *(Mark 3:21,31-35, 6:1-6).* The unbelief of Jesus' brothers (like that of the Pharisees) may have been partly due to Jesus' apparent laxity with regard to the Jewish Law – touching lepers and dead bodies, healing on the Sabbath – and because of his extravagant claims. So, while it is unlikely that Jesus suffered sustained opposition at home, it is clear that he endured the jibes of an uncomprehending family, so much so that he later specified his "own house" as not honouring him. However, years later, as we shall see, several members of his own extended family came to be among his most ardent disciples.

There can be little doubt that Joseph and Mary had trained their family in the highest standards of godliness. This can be seen, for example, in the remarkable reputation for prayerfulness which James, the brother of Jesus, gained as leader of the Jerusalem church. Their parents had clearly modelled a lifestyle of prayerfulness to their children. The early Christian writer Hegesippus tells us James was in the habit of entering the Temple alone, and was often found upon bended knees, interceding for the forgiveness of the people; so that "his knees became as hard as camels' ... And indeed, on account of his exceeding piety, he was called the Just."

The letter of James in the New Testament provides us with a window into the mind of its author and his concern for fellow Jewish Christians. It reflects the long and rich heritage of wisdom literature, but more importantly, is indebted greatly to his elder brother's wisdom. Much of the teaching in what we now refer to as the Sermon on the Mount *(Matthew 5-7, Luke 6)* can be seen mirrored in this pastoral letter.

The activities of Jesus' childhood are left mainly to our imagination, except for the record of one significant incident as a twelve-year-old in the Temple *(Luke 2:41-52).* The absence of other details points all the more to the assumption that his boyhood years were unremarkable and normal. We sometimes baulk at the thought of ordinariness, equating it with dullness and the drabness of a mediocre existence, but these silent years 'sanctified' ordinariness. The tendency to seek excitement as a means of escaping the mundane has caused some to suppose that Jesus'

---

[72] In *John 2:16-17*, Jesus referenced a messianic psalm, referring to the Temple. The same psalm also states, "I have become estranged from my brothers, and an alien to my mother's sons." *(Psalm 69:8).*

childhood was surely more thrilling and supernatural. This in turn has spawned a number of vivid, imaginative stories of the Christ child's miraculous exploits.

From childhood to adulthood, Jesus "increased in wisdom and stature, and in favour with God and man" *(Luke 2:52)*. Eight Hebrew terms were used by the Jews to describe the stages of a child's development. *Yeled*, a newborn baby *(Isaiah 9:6)*; *Yoneq*, a nursing baby *(Isaiah 11:8)*; *Odel*, the baby becoming ready to start on solid foods *(Lamentations 4:4)*; *Gamul*, the weaned child *(Isaiah 28:9)*; *Taph*, the child clinging to its mother *(Jeremiah 40:7)*; *Elem*, the stripling, a child becoming firm *(1 Samuel 17:56)*; *Naar*, the lad, one who shakes himself free, or youth *(Genesis 21:12)*; and *Bachur*, the ripened one, young man *(Judges 14:10)*. At each stage, we can imagine that Jesus grew to refer every thought and feeling to his heavenly Father in a way that was appropriate to his age, and in a way that was neither aloof nor super-spiritual, a quality that alienates rather than attracts, for he was "without sin" *(Hebrews 4:15)*.

These 'silent years' were to be an important period of preparation for Jesus, of storing away truth in the secret place of the heart, as his mother had also learned to do *(Luke 2:19)*. The years passed, a passage of time so crucial for the transformation of God-child to God-man; a time that could not, should not, be hurried. Jesus willingly embraced the commonplace, submitting to 'the trivial round, the common task'.

Might we adapt Paul's famous words to incorporate Jesus' awareness of God *(1 Corinthians 13:11-12)*?

> When Jesus was a child, he used to speak like a child, think like a child, reason like a child; when he became a man, he did away with childish ways. For then he saw in a mirror dimly, but now – ascended to the Father – he sees face to face; then he knew in part, but now he knows fully just as he was fully known before he came on earth.

CHAPTER SEVEN

Uprising in Galilee

The past is a foreign country. They do things differently there.[73]

L. P. Hartley

It is not difficult to conclude that Jesus lived in a time that was dangerous for Jews.[74]

Ben Witherington III

Six million of the eight million Jews of Jesus' day lived outside Israel under Parthian[75] rather than Roman rule. The Jewish homeland covered considerably more territory than the modern state of Israel, larger even than Solomon's kingdom, which had extended both sides of the Jordan River to the Dead Sea, and north to Damascus into present day Lebanon and Syria.[76] In 63 BC the emperor Pompey had claimed Jerusalem, bringing it under the sphere of Rome's influence. 26 year later, Herod the Great, with the backing of Rome, captured the city from Antigonus II Mattathius and was appointed king of Judea by the Romans. During the first century, Israel had a quick succession of firebrand leaders who set themselves up as the deliverers of their country and sometimes even as Messiah.

These were volatile times, and one notable incident took place when Jesus was about 11 or 12 years old, not far from where he lived. Around 6 or 7AD Judas of Gamala led a resistance to the census imposed for

---

[73] L. P. Hartley, *The Go-Between,* 1953
[74] Ben Witherington III, *The Jesus Quest; The Third Search for the Jew of Nazareth,* 16
[75] The Parthians (247BC-224AD) held sway over an empire that is now Iran and Iraq and were followers of Zoroastrianism and Babylonian religion.
[76] Charlotte Allen, *The Human Christ,* 126

Roman tax purposes by Quirinius in the Province of Judea *(Acts 5:37)*.[77] Judas marched on Sepphoris, a large and significant city about three miles north of Nazareth, seized weapons from the royal arsenal there, and for a brief time triumphed. According to Josephus, he told his countrymen they "would be cowards if they would endure to pay a tax to the Romans" and thus "submit to mortal men as their lords", when tribute should be paid to God alone. He encouraged Jews not to register and those who did had their houses burned and their cattle stolen by his followers. It is thought that Judas joined forces with a Pharisee named Zaddok to launch what was called the "Fourth Philosophy", otherwise known as Zealots or *Sicarii*, dagger men[78]. (The other three 'Philosophies' being the Pharisees, Sadducees, and Essenes.[79]) Rebelling against the governing Roman authorities, Judas proclaimed the Jewish state as a republic which recognised God alone as king and ruler, and his laws as supreme. The revolt continued to spread, and serious conflicts ensued.

Some scholars identify Judas of Gamala with Judas, son of Hezekiah the Zealot, who, according to Josephus, led the revolt in the time of Quintilius Varus the Roman general.[80] Varus advanced with two legions and with the help of Arab auxiliaries dispersed the Galilean rebels, defeated them, burned Sepphoris to the ground, and sold its inhabitants into slavery. He then marched into Judea, caught up the groups of patriots and had about 2,000 crucified – including Judas. Some 6,000 young Galileans were deported to slavery in the western empire. Concerning the backlash against the revolt in Sepphoris, Jack Nelson-Pallmeyer observes:

> The grisly scene of human remains nailed to crosses lining the
> roadways was part of Rome's psychological warfare, a

---

[77] Flavius Josephus, *Jewish War* 2.433 and *Jewish Antiquities* 18.1-10 and 18.23. Publius Sulpicius Quirinius (c.51BC-21AD) was appointed governor of Syria which included the province of Judea.

[78] The *Sicarii* were a splinter group of the Zealot movement. They carried *sicae* – small daggers concealed in their cloaks ready to attack Romans and their supervisors and then to blend in with the crowds undetected.

[79] Reza Aslan, *Zealot: The Life and Times of Jesus of Nazareth*, 40-41. The Zealots are not to be confused with the Zealot Party that arose 60 years later, after the Jewish Revolt in 66AD.

[80] *Jewish Encyclopedia, www.jewishencyclopedia.com/articles/9032-judas-the-galilean*

deterrent to future protesters. Varus then burned the city to the ground.[81]

This, then, was the backdrop to Jesus' years growing up in Nazareth: a time of ferment, bloodshed, and cruelty. Where scripture is silent, what Jesus witnessed or experienced as a youth remains a matter of conjecture. We can, however, weigh the evidence, balance probabilities and possibilities, and draw tentative conclusions – allowing that others may beg to differ. Let us consider the following as we seek to make reasonable suppositions from the known historical facts previously described.

Fact 1: The main highway linking Damascus to the Mediterranean coast and Egypt ran close to the town of Nazareth where Jesus spent his early life. It is reasonable to deduce that this thoroughfare would serve as an effective conduit of news and communication in the region.

Fact 2: Sepphoris was the largest city in the region (though not mentioned in the Bible) and the district capital of old Galilee. It was located a mere hour's walk from Nazareth. We may surmise therefore that news about events in Sepphoris would quickly be known in Nazareth.

Fact 3: Judas the Galilean led the uprising and tax rebellion against the Romans during the time when Jesus was a child living in the area. We may reason that Joseph's family would have known of the revolt and the severity with which it was crushed. Indeed, some of those fleeing Sepphoris quite possibly came through Nazareth and described their experiences. From the hilltops the family would have seen the town ablaze, witnessed the fleeing residents, heard about, or even seen, the mass crucifixions which took place by way of punishment and reprisal. These were traumatic events for anyone at any age. No doubt, as they heard their elders discussing, Jesus' contemporaries would talk among themselves about these grave matters. Were the Zealots right? Should they resist the occupying forces? What took place must have been the main talking point for many months. After the smoke and ashes had long disappeared and calm was restored, the fear and uncertainty would have lingered; the events seared onto the collective consciousness of all who witnessed them.

---

[81] Jack Nelson-Pallmeyer, *Jesus against Christianity: reclaiming the missing Jesus,* 189

Theory: Local people lived in a climate of fear, especially when the Roman military machine turned against them; but perhaps this, or other unrecorded incidents, persuaded some to become collaborators with the occupying forces (such as Matthew the tax collector) or some to become terrorists (like Simon the Zealot). Others might have chosen to lie low and attract as little attention as possible, hoping the Romans would not turn on them. Yet others may have whispered sedition and banded together to form a resistance movement. Some of those who were sent to slavery in the west (mostly to Spain and Sardinia) may have been known to locals. What impression would this have left upon Jesus? Would these have been in his mind when he later spoke of "the lost sheep of the house of Israel" *(Matthew 10:6)*?

Growing up under an oppressive military dictatorship, Jesus had time to think about these issues. We can imagine that such incidents may well have caused Jesus, as he talked to God his Father, to process carefully his own thoughts on important matters, such that 'what's hidden in the roots is later revealed in the shoots'. For example, his later teachings about paying taxes to Caesar showed incredible wisdom: "Render to Caesar the things that are Caesar's and to God the things that are God's" *(Mark 12:17)*. Despite an awareness of the causes that sparked the revolt, was this clear proof of his persuasion against the use of force "to resist him who is evil" *(cf. Matthew 5:39)*? "All those who take up the sword, shall perish by the sword" *(Matthew 26:52)*. Perhaps the radical seeds of non-violence notable in Jesus' teaching were sown as he witnessed the horror and futility of violent conflict and brutality.

Fact 4: Herod Antipas, the youngest son of Herod the Great, soon rebuilt Sepphoris. He lived there as tetrarch of Galilee and Perea until he founded a new capital for his principality at Tiberias, on the western shore of the lake (22AD). His massive urban building project at Sepphoris included a 15,000-seat theatre; many workers would have been required for this government-sponsored project.

We can reasonably deduce that this must have had a major impact on the economy of southern Galilee – the surrounding villages and towns such as Nazareth. Since builders and carpenters would have been required for decades, Sepphoris was the place where Joseph, and later perhaps Jesus, may well have earned their income as craftsmen or day labourers.[82]

A cautionary word: We also need to ask ourselves, when does something become a speculation too far? For example, consider the following line of reasoning. Traditionally, it is thought that Mary's parents were Joachim and Anna who lived in Sepphoris. If indeed Joseph did work in the city, perhaps he met Mary and her parents on one of his 'work trips'. While this offers a perfectly plausible scenario, it illustrates how, when traditions of uncertain historical validity, often documented centuries after an alleged incident took place, are combined with two or more sets of possible circumstances, the results can be little more than educated guesswork – appropriate perhaps for a historical novel but not to be relied upon. Therefore, at the same time as gleaning plausible insights to help us imagine events in a way that brings to life historical narrative, care and due regard also need to be exercised. It is this kind of care that I myself am seeking to exercise.

---

[82]   It seems improbable that there would have been sufficient work in Nazareth to sustain the family business and so economic necessity may have motivated them to work in Sepphoris – however much they might have disliked to.

CHAPTER EIGHT

Growing in Wisdom

What was working in Jesus was ... too vast and too sacred for any discussion of it, even with his mother. And perhaps he himself was at this time only as yet beginning to understand, and even then, but dimly, all that it meant.[83]

John Oxenford

Continue in what you have learned and have become convinced of, because you know those from whom you learned it, and how from infancy you have known the holy scriptures, which are able to make you wise for salvation.

2 Timothy 3:14-15

The Aramaic inscription on an ossuary discovered in Jerusalem created a sensation around the world when displayed in 2002. A thorough investigation supported the claim that the ossuary was indeed a genuine first century box into which the bones were placed one year after death. Opinions have differed though as to whether the inscription on the side is genuine.[84] It reads "*Ya'akov* son of *Yosef,* brother of *Yeshuah*" – James, son of Joseph, brother of Jesus. For some time, the ossuary's owner didn't realise that this might be the James, Joseph, and Jesus of the New Testament. Later it was pointed out to him that while these were all popular names in the first century, the combination of all three, and the unusual mention of the brother, could make this the first archaeological evidence for Jesus' existence. The owner had failed to make the connection. In a different context, Gentile believers often fail to make a connection by not appreciating the Jewish roots of their Christian faith.

---

[83] John Oxenford, *The Hidden Years*

[84] For a brief summary of the arguments for and against its genuineness: *https://christianpublishinghouse.co/2017/06/02/the-james-ossuary-the-earliest-witness-to-jesus-and-his-family/*

The Gospels are self-consciously Jewish – more so than we often imagine. By tapping into the rich vein of Jesus' Jewish heritage, we can appreciate more fully the 'secret years' of his life. Just as these days our social media interaction builds up a profile identity that provides a picture of our values, preferences, lifestyle, and even personality, to a certain extent it is possible to reconstruct a person's probable childhood and youth based on the social and historical background of their times. It is therefore helpful for us to investigate the influences to which Jesus was exposed as a boy. A formative influence upon Jesus' family, for example, would have been their observance of the five books of Moses, the *Torah*. As devout Jews, they would have paid tithes, kept the Sabbath, circumcised male family members, attended the synagogue regularly, and observed relevant purity laws. Mary and Joseph upheld days of purification in relation to childbirth and menstruation *(Luke 2:39)* and would have kept the dietary code and other aspects of the Torah which applied to daily life.

According to the Jewish world view, there is no division between the secular and the sacred; everything in the world is God's good creation. Even its most earthly aspects are joined to the divine, and observant Jews, like Joseph and his family, would have carried out the prescriptions of the Law, not only in the synagogue, but in their own home. Here there were countless occasions when Joseph would utter one of the many benedictions. Every action, no matter how commonplace, called forth a father's blessing, and every casual action and event was an occasion to thank and glorify God. There were, for example, 100 *berakhot*, or benedictions, that all Jews were required to pronounce between sunrise and sunset. "Like the 100 sockets which held up the sanctuary in the wilderness, so the 100 daily *berakhot* hold up the sanctuary of life," taught the rabbis, the Jewish scholars qualified to interpret the Law.

There were blessings upon awakening, for the humblest of bodily actions, and before meals; approximately one blessing every ten waking minutes. At the close of the Sabbath, the *havadalah* would have been recited:

> Blessed are you, O Lord our God, King of the universe, who makes a distinction between holy and profane, between light and darkness, between Israel and the nations, between the seventh day and the six working days. Blessed are you, O Lord, who makes a distinction between holy and profane.

How comprehensively Joseph pronounced such blessings we cannot know, but it is reasonable to suppose that many were part of Jesus' everyday experience growing up. Within the family home, Jesus was made aware of a universe dedicated to God, where each thought and action was coloured by a consciousness of God's presence, interest, and involvement.

What would Jesus' education have been like? Long before he was old enough to begin formal schooling, he would have learned Jewish culture and teachings from the many customs integrated into family life. There were the weekly rituals surrounding the Sabbath, and the daily act of morning prayer. For the latter, Joseph would bind on his left arm and forehead the phylacteries or *tephillin*, small boxes containing scriptural verses on folded slips of parchment: *Exodus 13:1-16, Deuteronomy 6:4-9* and *11:13-21*. Jesus must have asked about these and Joseph may have replied in the words of the Shema in *Deuteronomy 6:5-8*, that he was fulfilling God's command, and explained to Jesus the reasons for doing this.

Similarly, each year at Passover, Joseph would have explained to his family why they were eating unleavened bread and feasting *(Exodus 13:6-8)*. Another occasion to explain God's Law presented itself when the family would have built booths to live in during the Feast of Tabernacles. From his earliest years Jesus would have had many opportunities at home to learn about his heritage; and these would have been reinforced and supplemented at the synagogue.

Following the traditions and customs of the Jews, Joseph would have taken Jesus to the synagogue; in Hebrew, the *beth knesset* – the village house of assembly and prayer. He would almost certainly have attended at least three times a week: on the Sabbath and two other days, Monday and Thursday, when the Torah was read. In addition, he would have attended the anniversaries that form a compendium of Jewish theology on traditional holidays. These are essentially re-enactments in which the past events of God's people are remembered and relived. The Passover was the crowning point of the year, calling to mind the flight from Egypt and the end of Israel's slavery. These and the other festivals *(Leviticus 23)*, as we shall see, had a profound effect upon Jesus and were to become central to his perception of himself and his role.

The synagogue (Greek meaning literally "the gathering place"),would have been at the centre of Jesus' life as a boy, serving as a place of worship, as school, and also local law court. In a room adjoining the synagogue was the *beth hassepher*, the house of the Book; its purpose, to teach the written Law or Torah. A meal and an afternoon Bible study would have followed the Sabbath morning worship service. Here, systematic instruction was given and attendance was compulsory. Jewish traditions were faithfully preserved, and the education and values parents wanted their children to receive were passed on.

In ancient times study was considered to be one of the highest forms of worship *(cf. 2 Timothy 2:15)*. "A child ought to be fattened with the Torah as an ox is fattened in the stall," taught the rabbis. As God-fearing parents, conscious of the prophetic words, dreams, and visions they had received about their son, alongside their appreciation for their rich Jewish heritage, Joseph and Mary would have undoubtedly made participation in these activities a priority for Jesus.[85]

Hebrew education differed from that of other societies by beginning with God, the abstract and unseen, not with the seen and the concrete. It was spiritual and therefore quite different from the empirical and naturalistic systems of surrounding nations. It stressed acquiring the fear of the Lord and obedience to the Law, rather than reading and writing skills. Truth was deduced from the fact of God's existence, and not learned by induction.

In one ancient collection of Jewish writings that make up the basis of Jewish religious law, *The Palestinian Talmud,* it is recorded that Simon ben Shetah (c.100 BC) ordered that children from the age of five or six attend elementary school. Rabbi Joshua ben Gamala (high priest c.63-65BC and martyred under Herod the Great) decreed that teachers of children be appointed in every district and town. Rabbinic tradition tells us that families were not allowed to live in a place where there was no school. Every community with 25 boys was required to have one scribe

---

[85] By contrast with the picture painted here, levels of literacy were otherwise low in Middle Eastern societies where women were discriminated against and were not taught to read and write, and few men had the need to, particularly in rural areas such as Nazareth. Some estimate literacy as low as 3-5%, in which case Jesus was unusual in being able to read and write. Since understanding the Hebrew scriptures was so foundational to his development, we can assume that he and his parents made it a priority, which might not have been the case with other boys his age. Three texts indicate Jesus' ability to read and write: *Luke 4:16-30; John 7:15, 8:6.* All Jewish young men who had parents who were religious learned these skills in synagogue schools. Meir Bar-Ilan, *Illiteracy in the Land of Israel in the First Centuries C.E., https://faculty.biu.ac.il/~barilm/illitera.html*

or teacher. If there were more than 40 the scribe should be assisted by the *hazzan*, the synagogue official, who was also employed to look after the scrolls of scripture.

What might a typical school day for Jesus have been like? The first session would begin about sunrise, with another in the late afternoon. So Jesus would have been at the synagogue every day of the week, sometimes attending twice a day for several hours at a time. There were no vacations, and there was a saying that children must not be kept from going to school, even for building the Temple. School was not suspended on the Sabbath, though there were restrictions as to what might be taught on that day. (A new passage could not be studied for the first time on the Sabbath, but it was permitted to make a first revision, which appears to mean that mistakes in learning the passage might be corrected.)

The teaching style was geared to a culture of oral tradition, in which the spoken word was passed from one generation to the next. Jesus, with other boys his age, would have sat cross-legged at the feet of their teacher in a semi-circle on the floor to learn the Torah. He would have begun by tracing out the 22 letters of the Hebrew alphabet, then progressed to individual words, then whole phrases from the Torah, his only reading material. Like his contemporaries, Jesus was taught to read so that as an adult he could read God's word in the synagogue.

The only writing we can for certain attribute to Jesus was when, as an adult, he traced words in the dust at the feet of a woman accused of adultery *(John 8:1-11)*. We know the impact of those words on the bystanders, but what he actually wrote has been a matter for conjecture ever since. What this incident does provide us with, however, is evidence that Jesus knew how to write – just as an earlier incident confirms that he could read *(Luke 4:16)*. Incidentally, it is interesting that Jesus, the subject of more books than anyone who has ever lived, was never to write one himself. In the context of his mission, it was perhaps not so much writing but being able to read that was important for Jesus. His reading and study of the scriptures in school provided a solid foundation for his life's work. He had chosen "to live by every word that proceeds from the mouth of God" *(Matthew 4:4)*, as we shall explore further.[86]

The school textbook was the Torah, or Pentateuch, the first five books of the Hebrew scriptures, beginning with the creation story *(Genesis 1-5)*, and the chief task for the students was to memorise the

---

[86] See chapter 16, *Treasures Old and New*

Levitical law *(Leviticus 1-8)*. As a young boy, Jesus would also have learned by heart *Numbers 15:37-41*, the *Shema (Deuteronomy 6:4-9, 11:13-21)* and the *Hallel (Psalms 113-118)*. Learning to read and write the Hebrew script were essential basics of the curriculum, along with arithmetic – useful for the custom of tithing and for business transactions.

In advice that wouldn't be out of place today, Rabbi Akiba urged:

> The teacher should strive to make the lesson agreeable to the pupils by clear reasons, as well as by frequent repetitions, until they thoroughly understand the matter, and can recite it with great fluency.

Memorization was an important skill, and those who could commit many passages to memory often became outstanding scholars. This was all the more important because it was not considered appropriate, except for teaching and liturgical purposes, to make copies of the sacred words of the Torah. The schoolroom and the narrow streets around it would have echoed daily with the rhythmic chanting of boys memorising their lessons.

> At five years one comes to the study of scripture; at ten to the Mishnah; at 13 years to the fulfillment of the commandments; at 15 to the Talmud.
>
> *[Mishnah with commentary] (Aboth m Ab. 5.21)*

Each marked a passage of rites in Jewish tradition. Like other Jewish boys, Jesus would have been viewed as reaching manhood at 13 years of age.

By the age of ten Jesus would have had a thorough knowledge of the five books of Moses, and would then advance to the *beth talmud*, the house of learning, to supplement his knowledge of the written law by a more complex oral form (later written down as the *Mishnah*). The curriculum featured the memorization of more Jewish laws, those having to do with agriculture, feasts, festivals, marriage and divorce, civil and criminal law, animal sacrifices at the Temple, and laws of purity and impurity. A further "house of study" was known as *beth midrash*, where learning became yet more challenging. It was said:

> 1,000 boys go the school house to learn to read the scripture and only 100 go out of it. 100 go on to study the Mishnah and

only 10 go further; 10 go to the study of the Talmud and only one of them completes it.

Midrash Leviticus Rabba II

Generations of rabbis explained, clarified, and adapted the principles of the Torah to everyday situations and problems, and their wisdom was passed on in morning and evening sessions. Students who attended at this level would gather around their teacher, take part in question and answer sessions, and finally repeat the lesson until the exact wording was imprinted on their minds.

Sending children to school was a focus of national pride. In social standing teachers were second only to rabbinical scholars, and the school was held in highest regard as a symbol of all that education meant to a Jew. The standards were exceptionally high. Exactly how far Jesus continued his education can only be a matter of speculation. Economic pressure may have required him to leave his studies and work with his father. By the time Jesus attended his first pilgrimage to Jerusalem at the age of 12 we can be almost certain that he would have enjoyed a foundation of seven years of school education in the synagogue.

Joseph may have told Jesus even before he was 12 that he was not his biological father, since Jesus, as we shall see, refers to the Temple as his "Father's house" *(Luke 2:42-50).* So did Jesus experience an increasing sense of detachment from the preoccupations of others his age – a feeling of not belonging, since he could not share their priorities or ambitions? Years later, Peter would come to appreciate that on earth he was a "foreigner and exile" *(1 Peter 2:11),* a conviction shared by other early Christians: "Here we do not have an enduring city, but we are looking for the city that is to come" *(Hebrews 13:14).*[87] We can suppose that this feeling was most probably felt even more keenly by Jesus. From his years of studying the scriptures, Jesus would have come increasingly to realise the uniqueness of his calling.

Around this time, a lay movement sprang up across Galilee and Judea called the *haberim* (literally 'the friends'). The name was taken from *Psalm 119:63:* "I am a friend *[haber]* to all who fear you, to all who follow your precepts." In its devotion to understanding the Law, the group had much in common with the Pharisees, and in towns and

---

[87] This theme developed in Hebrews confirms our status as outsiders in this world *(11:10,16, 12:22),* but heirs of what will be far better *(10:34, 11:13).*

villages, serious-minded Jews would gather after their day's labour for discussions, studying the Torah and applying its laws to their lives. Kenneth Bailey explains:

> A young Jew in his early teens had the option of joining such a group. If he decided to do so, he was committed to becoming a "student of the rabbis" and participating in their discussions. Those Jews who wished to spend their spare time in activities other than scholarly debates were not a part of these associations ... With this pattern of culture in mind, it is easy to assume that Jesus went on to spend eighteen years in sustained discussion with the brightest and best thinkers in Nazareth and the surrounding villages.

Bailey is confident Jesus could well have been part of such a group since we read in the Gospels that he demonstrates skills in the rabbinic style of debate as would have been nurtured in these fellowships.[88] From the age of 30, Jesus would demonstrate time and again during his public ministry a considerable ability in the rabbinic style of debating. It is therefore not surprising that the community came to recognise his wisdom and gifts, calling him "Rabbi". But, as we are seeing, the journey beforehand was carefully ordained and willingly embraced, as Jesus optimised every opportunity to learn, to grow, to develop in a way that was pleasing to his Father, and would ultimately accomplish God's plans and purposes on earth.

---

[88] Kenneth E. Bailey, *Jesus and the Prodigal: How Jesus Retold Israel's Story*, 24-25

CHAPTER NINE

Passover in Jerusalem

Every year Jesus' parents went to Jerusalem for the Festival of Passover. When he was twelve years old, they went up to the festival, according to the custom.

Luke 2:41

The flow of Gospel narrative concerning the life of Jesus takes us from Nazareth to Bethlehem to Egypt, and then back to Nazareth in about 3BC. Before we pick up the story again in about 26AD, it is hidden except for one brief episode – Jesus and his family went to Jerusalem in about 7AD for the Passover *(Luke 2:41-52)*.[89] This annual spring festival celebrating the deliverance from Egyptian slavery brought large crowds to Jerusalem; those unable to make the journey would mark the occasion with their families at home. Susan Haber comments:

> It is likely that only a small percentage of Jews living in the land of Israel, and an even smaller percentage of Diaspora Jews, went up to Jerusalem for every pilgrimage feast. This modified observance probably emerged as a response to practical issues of feasibility with respect to time, economic resources and physical capability. The commandment to make pilgrimage thus became an indeterminate one, which was kept by each individual according to his piety, his strength and his means.[90]

Jesus would have first engaged with Israel's history through the didactic reading of the Pentateuch in the synagogue each Sabbath, but also through the Jewish festivals commemorated in the form of re-

---

[89] The text is ambiguous as to whether this was Jesus' first visit to Jerusalem.
[90] Susan Haber, *Going Up to Jerusalem: Purity, Pilgrimage and the Historical Jesus* in ed. Adele Reinhartz, *They Shall Purify Themselves. Essays on Purity in Early Judaism,* 184

enactments – opportunities to revive and relive Israel's past in a series of religious holidays. *Rosh Hashanah* commemorates the creation; Passover, *Pesach*, the exodus from Egypt; Pentecost, *Shavuot*, the gift of the Law; Tabernacles, *Sukkôth*, "booths", the time in the wilderness and God's goodness to Israel. There were other minor festivals but Luke alone records Jesus attending one of the most important – Passover.[91]

Jesus would have heard the Passover story from the time when he was old enough to join his parents at a meal, and would have asked the traditional question at the meal table, "Why is this night different from all other nights?" He would have questioned Joseph, "What does this ceremony mean to you?" *(Exodus 12:26)*. The purpose of the evening meal, the *Seder,* was to call vividly to mind the flight from Egypt and the end of Israel's bondage. We can wonder whether, on Jesus' first pilgrimage to Jerusalem, he may have first made the connection between the Passover lamb and his own future role as the Lamb of God who would take away the sins of the world *(John 1:29)*.

From Nazareth, Jesus would have been accustomed to seeing fires lit on the surrounding hills every month, heralding the coming of the new moon. He would have learned that these beacons linked a chain originating on the Mount of Olives, in Jerusalem, where priests lit the first one. To Jesus that far-off place must have seemed like the centre of the world, the earthly habitation of the God of history, where even the calendar dates had their origin. Yet we can wonder what he really felt on his first arrival, observing the stark contrast between Jewish and Roman worlds, so far apart culturally and spiritually from his normal village surroundings. It must have been a shock.

The occasion recorded by Luke occurred shortly before Jesus was thirteen; old enough to take on the 'yoke of the Torah', the point at which he assumed responsibility for his own observance of the Law, and the beginning of his adult life of study, reflection, and observance.

According to the first century Jewish historian Josephus, it was not obligatory for women to attend the Passover in Jerusalem but was common for them to do so. He mentions one particular occasion when

---

91 As an adult, Jesus continued to go up to Jerusalem to celebrate Passover *(John 12:12; Mark 14:12-26)*. Jesus also kept Tabernacles *(John 7:1-39)*. *John 10:22-23* may also indicate that Jesus celebrated the *Hanukkah* festival which commemorated the C2 BC rededication of the Temple under the Maccabees.

"all the people ran together out of the villages to the city, and celebrated the festival, having purified themselves with their wives and children, according to the law."[92] How often Mary had made that pilgrimage before we cannot tell. We read of Mary being only with her husband and responsible oldest son in Luke's account.

Josephus indicates that the quickest route from Galilee to Jerusalem was a three-day journey through Samaria. In the time of Jesus, this journey represented a walk through history, with reminders on the 150-mile round trip of events of national and spiritual importance. As was the custom of many pilgrims, Jesus and his family probably walked around the northern side of Jerusalem to enter the Temple area from the eastern gate. From the Mount of Olives, the 'hill of anointing', Jesus would have glimpsed the splendour of the gleaming gold and marble of Herod's Temple. By that time Jerusalem had attained its maximum size before it would be eventually destroyed in 70AD by the Romans. It now had a three-mile circumference: the ancient city King David had captured from the Jebusites to the south-east and, to the north, the new city on Mt Zion where the Temple was built. Between the two hills, Jebus and Zion, a new settlement had developed uniting the two parts of the city. Finally, a new section had grown up along the ravine formed by the Brook Kidron.

The Babylonian Talmud, a compilation of Jewish laws and ethics written at the end of the fifth century AD, states:

> He who has not seen Jerusalem in her splendor, has never seen
> a desirable city in his life. He who has not seen the Temple in
> its full construction has never seen a glorious building in his
> life.[93]

The Temple was considered the "centre of the nations" *(Ezekiel 5:5)*, half earthly, half heavenly in nature, the meeting point of two horizons, one immanent, one transcendent. Built on the rocky, muddy, earthy "promised land" it was considered "a counterpart of the inaccessible sanctuary that the Messiah might be on the point of approaching"[94].

---

[92] Flavius Josephus, *Antiquities of the Jews,* 11.109
[93] *Baba Bathra 4a*
[94] Robert Aron, *A Boy Named Jesus, How the Early Years Shaped His Life* 87, 126-127

By contrast, from the Temple Jesus would have seen the merchants and moneychangers and have been aware, too, of the Roman soldiers keeping watch from the tower of Antonia, which towered over the Temple – inspecting everyone who came into the precincts. These were salutary reminders that all was not as it should be; the city, indeed the whole country, was under the domination of Gentiles.

All around, a city of tents would have emerged, temporary housing for pilgrims celebrating the Passover. Joseph's family would have joined others in this joyful experience. For the festival week, Jerusalem's population of 55,000 might swell to a quarter of a million or more at this time, as pilgrims flocked from across the Roman Empire to the 35-acre site of the Temple, the House of God.[95] (We can imagine the scene, perhaps not unlike contemporary music festivals.) Twenty chapters and twenty years separate the accounts in Luke's Gospel of Jesus' first and last Passover celebrations *(Luke 2, 22)*.[96] Both omit any mention of the event that had dominated the occasion for over 1,000 years – the lambs that were sacrificed at this time of remembrance, thanksgiving, and hope.

Each family would bring or purchase a lamb for the festival, older than eight days but younger than a year. It is debatable whether in New Testament times an individual family member would slaughter the family's lamb, as the Law prescribed, or whether it was the monopoly of the priests. Traditionally, boys like Jesus, aged twelve or thirteen, assumed the role of adulthood by taking on this responsibility. This would have been a defining moment in Jesus' transition from boyhood to manhood. *Pirkei Avot,* a book of Jewish ethical instruction, taught that at thirteen a child comes to the "age of fulfilment", that eighteen was the proper age for marriage, and twenty the time he should earn a livelihood.

---

[95] Estimates of pilgrims range from 125,000 (Jeremias) to 300,000 (E. P. Sanders). Susan Haber, *Going Up to Jerusalem: Purity, Pilgrimage and the Historical Jesus* in ed. Adele Reinhartz, *They Shall Purify Themselves. Essays on Purity in Early Judaism,* 181.

[96] John offers more information regarding Jesus' travels, recounting at least four pilgrimages: twice for Passover *(John 2:13, 11:55)*, once for Tabernacles *(7:10)* and once for an unspecified feast *(5:1)*. "There is no indication that Jesus made the pilgrimage for every feast, although it is a possibility. It is more likely, however, that his pilgrimage practices resembled those of other Galilean Jews, who placed particular emphasis on attending the Passover feast." Susan Haber, 187.

In the third century AD, this ritual became the basis for the *Bar Mitzvah* – when a boy became a "son of the commandment". In the Priests' Court, rows of priests held silver or gold bowls and stood between the altar and the Jewish men who had come to make sacrifices. Each Israelite, including young boys entering manhood, stood with his offering and cut its throat. A priest caught the blood in the bowl and passed it along the line of priests to be thrown against the base of the altar. The animal was then taken to the slaughtering tables and butchered; the fat was collected, salted, and burned on the altar fire. Then the rest of the animal's carcass was given to the family for the preparation of their Passover meal *(Exodus 12:3-14)*.

We don't know how Jesus felt at the sight of up to 30,000 lambs being killed in the Temple area on a single afternoon, or if it already had some special significance to him. Perhaps it was in order to discuss the meaning of this Festival with Israel's most learned men that the boy Jesus stayed behind in the Temple courts.

Commenting on the development of Jesus' faith from childhood to adolescence, Richard Kopf observes:

> Jesus, whether as an infant, child, adolescent or youth, grew and developed just the same as anyone else of his day and age. His growth was not only physical, but mental ("in wisdom"), and spiritual ("in God's favor" or "grace") just as that of any person in his or her early life. Other than this one single incident, there is no hint of anything special about him, at least in any sense that he was conscious of. And even here, allowing for the gospel writer's hindsight, there is nothing in this story to indicate anything different than a particular precocity and giftedness marking this older boy becoming a young man. Jesus is someone who bears special watching. He will be a marked man and that to some degree he already senses it, because for him God's "business" is the same as his "Father's" business and he seems more than eager to begin his apprenticeship.[97]

Who were these teachers of the Law that Jesus met with? In all likelihood, the majority were *Perushim* ('the separated ones', i.e.

---

[97]   Richard W. Kropf, *The Faith of Jesus – the Jesus of History and the Stages of Faith*, 22

67

Pharisees), but there were others: non-conformists, mystics, intellectuals, pure Jewish, patriotic, tradesmen and merchants, liberal in spirit, authoritative exponents of the Law who enjoyed the easy-going and democratic approach adopted in the synagogues. They delighted in engaging ceaselessly in the exegesis of the Torah, not allowing it to be monopolised by the priests but adapting it to the needs of ordinary people, and in so doing they multiplied the application of God's Law. There were good and bad among them, with Hillel, who was the head of an academy in Jerusalem between 40BC and 10AD, perhaps representing the best qualities of the Pharisees.[98]

The Talmud describes seven types of Pharisee including those "painted Pharisees" who pretended to be what they were not, whom Jesus later labelled hypocrites.[99] Luke records that the better ones among them sought to protect Jesus from Herod's wrath *(Luke 13:31-33)*, and casts Gamaliel, one of their number, in a favourable light *(Acts 5:34-39)*. Luke also aligns Paul among their number *(Acts 23:6-10)*.

Robert Aron invites us to imagine some of the events of Jesus' three days in the Temple in a passage that is worth quoting at length.

> Probably the doctors[100] received him in one of the rooms adjacent to the synagogue, which was secluded and quiet in contrast to the holiday clamor of the courts outside.*[101]* This was not a room set aside for study, but on tables or shelves along the walls, or perhaps even in a tabernacle, there were stacked scrolls bearing the sacred texts from Genesis to the Prophets. At intervals, the doctors went to look up a particular verse to support the point of view they were setting forth to the boys and young men before them. They were so familiar with the material that they found at once what they were looking for ...

---

[98] In opposition was a divergent branch of Pharisaic doctrine led by Shammai. Both represented the Talmudic tradition extending back to the time of Moses – Israel's great unwritten religious and literary compendium.

[99] The Pharisees prescribed 613 laws: 365 were negative (as many as the days of the year), 248 positive (as many, so they thought, as the muscles of the human body).

[100] i.e. doctors of the Law (rabbis)

[101] There was a synagogue area within the Temple complex.

But in spite of their learning the doctors were not mere pedants. Representatives of the holiday crowd came in at intervals to interrupt them. A beggar implored alms; a man of conscience came to resolve some moral problem that was on his mind; the head of a family questioned him about the details of his household Passover celebration: the proper hour at which to hold the Seder, the foods to be served, the order of the traditional questions and answers. All these matters were settled by consultation of the sacred scrolls around the walls, for both public life and private life were regulated by the Law. As Jesus approached these learned men he may well have felt a deepening and strengthening of the ties that bound him to the tradition of his fathers.

The doctors, with prayer shawls over their shoulders and prayer vests worn next to the skin, welcomed this opportunity to instruct the young. They were not members of the professional clergy; indeed, they had gainful occupations on the outside, for it was forbidden to make money from teaching the Torah. In the exercise of a spare-time priestly function they found a welcome release from worldly cares and also a source of spiritual satisfaction. They were happy to renew their intimacy with God, to deepen their understanding and to carry out the prescriptions of the Shema by teaching the commandments to their juniors.

To the young Nazarene their argumentation may at first have appeared unduly difficult, requiring a mental effort such as to bring on tension and fatigue. But their contagious enthusiasm, the joy they derived from the closely reasoned justification of a subtle Halakah, the peaceful assurance that rang out in their singsong declarations, all these facilitated Jesus' approach to their intellectual traditions.

Changing their pace, the doctors allowed their young hearers to relax momentarily the strained attentiveness required by the Halakah, and listen to the Haggadah.[102] Jesus could not have failed to notice the lesser emphasis they placed upon it. The

---

[102] the order of service used at Passover

> Halakah, which teaches the practical applications of the Torah, or in brief, God's word, must be strictly taught, so that there is no misunderstanding of the text.[103]

Jesus, we read, "was sitting among the teachers, listening to them and asking them questions. Everyone who heard him was amazed at his understanding and his answers" *(Luke 2:46-47)*; such wisdom was remarkable in one so young, and perhaps even beyond what they themselves had gleaned from decades of devotion to the Law and Prophets. The question and answer format to the discussion is typically Jewish; but what is so astounding is that Jesus is not only asking questions, as we might expect from someone his age, but he is also providing answers to questions of the rabbis. This perhaps took place, not over just one afternoon, but across three full days – a not inconsiderable length of time. In his Gospel, Mark records how 20 years later a delegation would come from Jerusalem to question Jesus about his teaching *(Mark 7:1-13)*. We may wonder whether any of these rabbis had been among those he had first met as a twelve-year-old.

After the week-long ceremony was over, Joseph and Mary had set off for home. Occupied with other matters, they felt no concern that they had not actually seen Jesus among the group, probably assuming he was walking with other relatives and fellow pilgrims. Any parent can easily imagine their anxiety when they realised Jesus was not in fact among their group of travellers. We can sense their sheer relief on returning to the city and finding their son in the Temple. Naturally, emotions spilled out as a rebuke after the strain of uncertainty; here he was, safe, among the rabbis in the Temple. Luke records Mary's perspective: "Son, why have you treated us like this? Your father and I have been anxiously searching for you" *(Luke 2:48)*. The words "son" and "father" seemed to have touched Jesus for his reply is gently corrective: "Didn't you know I had to be in my Father's house?" *(Luke 2:49)*. We sense Jesus wanted his mother to remember that Joseph was not his true earthly father and that his heavenly Father commanded even greater allegiance.

To speak of God as "my Father" was highly unusual for any individual, let alone a twelve-year-old, and illustrates the intimacy and uniqueness the Son enjoyed with God. The Spirit testified with his spirit

---

[103] Robert Aron, *A Boy Named Jesus: How the Early Years Shaped His Life*, 126-127

that he was God's child *(cf. Romans 8:15-16)*. There was much Mary did not yet understand, still more for her to ponder *(Luke 2:51)*. We also read that both parents were "astonished" *(Luke 2:48)*. It must have been a revelation to encounter that degree of understanding in their own child. What a lesson, from then on, they would be learning from their son, as he sought to help them understand for themselves more about his unique role.

In *Novo Millennio Ineunte*, Pope John Paul II wrote about Jesus in the Temple and the "frontier zone" of the mystery of the incarnation: Christ's self-awareness. Jack Dominian has sought to provide a perspective on the mind of Jesus from a psychological point of view. About this crucial episode in his life he writes:

> By the age of twelve, Jesus could distinguish between his earthly father and his heavenly Father, with the knowledge that he was the Son. We must presume that Jesus developed this self-understanding slowly. It did not come to him suddenly as a bolt from the sky ... By the age of twelve, and probably much earlier, he had made the separation from Joseph and had reconciled the two parts of his identity, while being clear which was the primary one ... A loving relationship with his human parents prepared Jesus for an understanding both of love and relationship, of being recognized, wanted, appreciated and belonging. All this enabled him to have an infrastructure for his relationship with his heavenly father. The task of his earthly parents was to prepare the background, to put no obstacles in his way, and to allow the special awareness of his identity to take root – even though they themselves simply did not understand his relationship with his heavenly Father, as the Temple episode shows. Psychologically, Jesus' upbringing was such that it put no obstacles in the way of his divine insights.[104]

From birth, the seed of Jesus' self-awareness germinated, growing to full maturity in adulthood. There may never have been a time when he thought of himself merely as a human being, nor that he had no inkling of his divine nature. Perhaps the three days after the Passover celebration

---

[104] Jack Dominian, *One Like Us: A Psychological Interpretation of Jesus*, 79-83

with the doctors of the Law deepened his understanding of his faith and served to awaken in him further a consciousness of his mission.

Nearly two more decades of shaping and preparation, of testing and forging, still lay ahead. Jesus must wait in perfect obedience for the right time to disclose his identity, attentive to that specific "hour", ordained for him since the foundation of the world.

Chapter Ten

Growing up in Galilee

In the future, he will honor Galilee of the nations, by the Way of the Sea, beyond the Jordan...

Isaiah 9:1

The sufferings caused by the pitiless tyranny of the Roman rulers, the heedlessness of the Herodian princes, the cowardice of the Jewish aristocracy, the sycophancy of the high priests and the discord among the various parties...[105]

Heinrich Graetz

Each year millions of tourists and pilgrims visit Israel, the land where Jesus lived, in the hope of deepening their understanding and appreciation of the person and the place where he lived. But in two millennia, much has changed. Naturally, there are now many large urban areas; yet surprisingly, some parts of Galilee may be more rural today than they were then. This can give the false impression that Jesus lived in a quiet village far removed from the hustle and bustle of city life.[106]

In the time of Jesus, Israel had a population between 500,000 and 700,000. There were a large number of both urban centres and village communities in lower Galilee, a region roughly 15 miles by 25 miles, making it one of the most densely populated areas of the country, indeed of the entire Roman Empire. According to Josephus there were 204

---

[105] Heinrich Graetz, *The History of the Jews from the earliest times to the present day*

[106] For a good introduction see, Stephen Travis' *The Galilee Jesus Knew*. See also David Landis, *Travel, Transportation and Movement in the First Century, www.nazarethvillage.com/discover/findings-research/first-century-travel/*

settlements in Galilee alone.[107] The four main valleys which cross lower Galilee formed excellent trade routes, running in the direction of the great coastal cities of Caesarea, Acco-Ptolemais, and Tyre. Life in this part of the country during the first century was as metropolitan as anywhere else in the empire.

> The picture that emerges for Galilee in the early first century is one of an essentially Jewish character shared with Judea. Thinly populated in the late second century BCE, Galilee saw an expansion in settlement under Hasmonean rule by settlers whose Jewish material culture is evident in excavated data … of stone vessels, *miqwaoth* or ritual baths, burials in *kokhim* shafts with ossuaries, and diet in which pork is absent. It is with this culture and with the demographic and social-economic stresses created by the new urbanization under Herod Antipas that Jesus' essentially "prophetic critique" resonates.[108]

Nazareth is now the capital and largest city in Northern District of Israel, with a population of over 75,000. At the time of Jesus, however, it was an insignificant settlement among Galilee's 200 villages, with an estimated population of between 100-400 people of two or three clans. It was small enough for everyone to know everyone else, but not large enough to sustain a livelihood for many who had to travel further afield to support their families.[109] Covering a mere 2.5 hectares, Nazareth was near one of the busiest trade routes of ancient Israel, being just six miles from the Via Maris, the main route from Egypt to Syria.

Much of Galilee was predominantly agricultural and so it is hardly surprising that Jesus was also familiar with country life.[110] In the time of Jesus, fellow villagers in Nazareth made their living by growing grapes, olives and grain on terraces cut into the limestone hills. At harvest time,

---

[107] Josephus has been regarded by historians as prone to exaggeration, and some of his claims open to question. Nevertheless, in this instance the number is thought to be accurate. Chaim Ben David, *Were there 204 settlements in Galilee at the time of Josephus Flavius?*

[108] James Boyce reviewing Jonathan L. Reed, *Archaeology and The Galilean Jesus,* 204, *https://wordandworld.luthersem.edu/content/pdfs/21-2_Africa/21-2_Reviews.pdf*

[109] For an idea of what the village looked like at the time: *www.nazareth.com*

[110] For example, *Luke 13:6-9, 15, 19, 21, 34*

all the villagers – Jesus likely included – would have trodden grapes to extract juice and huddled in watchtowers at night to guard their produce against thieves.[111] Even if Jesus and his father were busy with construction work much of the time, they likely would have joined the villagers at harvest time. Pfann and Murphy O'Connor write:

> At the time the crop came in, everyone put everything aside, whether he was a carpenter or did something else. Along with the others, Jesus might have crushed grapes with his bare feet and spent the nights in one of the towers – a small room on a tall stone base – with the villagers, telling stories, singing and playing the flute to pass the time.[112]

From childhood Jesus would have regularly heard the sound of Greek-speaking visitors as they passed through his village on business. It was also close to three major ancient cities. Tiberias was on the Sea of Galilee, Scythopolis on the main route to Jerusalem, and the ancient regional capital, Sepphoris, was less than an hour's walk away and clearly visible from most of the village. In Jesus' time, this city had become the administrative centre of the Roman provincial government.

When Jesus settled in Nazareth with his parents, he was perhaps two or three years old. This was after the death of seventy-year-old Herod the Great. His kingdom was divided up, and his shrewd and crafty son, Antipas, became Tetrarch of Galilee. Antipas' realm was limited, but his wealth and indulgence were clear to all. Jesus lived his boyhood, youth and adult years under the rule of this man whom he later called "that fox" *(Luke 13:32)* and warned his disciples against "the leaven of Herod Antipas" – his corruptive and corrosive influence *(Mark 8:15)*. No doubt, Antipas and his court made their impression upon Jesus' mind and imagination, since many of his parables refer to courtiers with soft clothes, banquets, and divided, warring kingdoms.

Jesus lived as a Jew in a highly cosmopolitan community where Jews and Gentiles lived in neighbouring communities and conducted business with each other. In "Galilee of the Gentiles" *(Isaiah 11:1)*, Jesus would

---

[111] These images emerge from excavations of the only pristine farmland left in the centre of modern Nazareth.

[112] Karin Laub, *New Archaeological Dig Sheds Light on Jesus' Boyhood in Nazareth.* See also: *Nazareth Dwelling Discovery May Shed Light on Boyhood of Jesus, https://www.theguardian.com/world/2009/dec/21/nazareth-dwelling-discovery-jesus*

have rubbed shoulders with many who shared neither his faith nor the rich tapestry of Jewish life and culture.

In this environment, he probably acquired the accent common to his fellow-Galileans. Peter's accent, for example, betrayed him as being one of his followers shortly after Jesus' arrest; "Of course, you are one of them," they said. "After all, the way you speak gives you away!" *(Matthew 26:73, cf. Acts 2:7)*. The snobbish southerners of Jerusalem were amused by the sloppiness of the Galileans in speaking Aramaic. The Talmud, for example, features a typical Galilean being ridiculed in the Jerusalem marketplace for trying to buy what he called *amar*. He was chided, "You stupid Galilean, do you want something to ride on [*hamar*: a donkey]? Or something to drink [*hamár*: wine]? Or something for clothing [*'amar*: wool]? Or something for a sacrifice [*immar*: a lamb]?" As Galileans, they spoke Aramaic with a strong accent and dropped the *aleph*, for example, 'Lazarus' instead of the more correct 'Alazar'.[113]

While there is no record in the Gospels of Jesus having visited Tiberias, Scythopolis, or Sepphoris, he may well have worked for some of the wealthy people who lived in these cities. In 3BC Herod Antipas had chosen Sepphoris as his capital, the "ornament of all Galilee" (Josephus). With a population of 30,000, it contained courts, a fortress, a 4,000-seat Greco-Roman Theatre, a palace, a colonnaded street on top of the acropolis, two city walls, two markets (upper and lower), archives, the royal bank, and the arsenal. As noted previously,[114] because of its proximity to Nazareth, it is easy to imagine that Joseph and Jesus were involved in some of Herod Antipas' grand building schemes in his new capital. Skilled construction workers were needed for ambitious projects like these.

The proximity of Sepphoris to Nazareth made it likely that Jesus was exposed to the full range of Greco-Roman culture. He would have needed Greek to communicate with the city's diverse population, one that included a large number of Gentiles. Antipas's construction projects could have created employment opportunities for a *tekton* like him, and the city, like others in the area, included many buildings characteristic of Greco-Roman urbanization – temples, bathhouses, a theatre, and other monumental architecture. Jesus might have sat in the theatre, watching

---

[113] See *John 11*
[114] Chapter 7, *Uprising in Galilee*

classical plays. He might also have heard popular philosophers preaching on the city's corners.[115]

Jesus was familiar with the theatre for he repeatedly used a word that has no equivalent in Hebrew or Aramaic. Seventeen times he refers to "hypocrites" – play-actors[116] who spoke behind a dramatic mask to conceal their true identity.

With the Sea of Galilee close by, Jesus would also have been very familiar with the fishing business. As the most prosperous segment of Galilee's economy, the fishing trade depended on boats constructed of wood and were often in need of repair. Jesus may well have been involved in this. One such boat dating from the first century AD was discovered in 1986 on the north-west shore at Kinnereth. Originally constructed of cedar, investigations showed it had been repaired with no less than ten other types of wood over the next century.

The shift after 19AD in Herodian construction projects to the area of Galilee may have led Jesus to seek work in this region. The discovery of the necropolis at Tiberias indicates that Jesus may have sought work in the ship repair yards at Migdal (Magdala), the major harbour on the west shore of Galilee. If he were an itinerant labourer it would have been natural to move round the lake from harbour to harbour. Might it have been that Jesus met (or was even employed by) the fishermen sons of Zebedee? This may certainly explain why the fishermen who became disciples followed him so quickly, if they had already met him and were aware of some of the things he said.

In his parables, Jesus describes, with fine attention to detail, kings, tax collectors, unscrupulous judges, crafty stewards, and self-confident Pharisees. Such a cast of characters is far removed from those that might be expected in rural Nazareth, which makes it probable that Jesus had worked in a cosmopolitan setting for some time.

Jesus and his contemporaries grew up knowing the cruel tyranny of the Roman occupation forces. Many Jews were either servants or slaves; and even for those who were not, life was hard. The ruling classes lived in comfortable affluence; the poor barely survived. Religious Studies professor John Dominic Crossan[117] describes the social hierarchy of the Roman Empire. At the top were the Ruler and the Governors. Together

---

[115] Mark A. Chancey, *Greco-Roman Culture & the Galilee of Jesus*, 5
[116] For example, *Matthew 6:2,5,16, 7:5, 15:7, 22:18, 23:13-15*
[117] J. D. Crossan, *Jesus, a Revolutionary Biography*

they made up only one per cent of the population but owned at least half of the land. Among the higher 'classes' were three other groups: Priests, who owned as much as fifteen percent of the land; the Retainers, ranging from military generals to expert bureaucrats; and the Merchants.

Further down the social scale were the Peasants who formed the vast majority of the population. About two-thirds of their annual crops went to support the upper classes. Those who were more fortunate lived at subsistence level on the harvest, just able to support themselves, their families, and livestock, with enough seed supply for the following year. Drought, debt, disease, or death would force unfortunate families off their own land and into share-cropping, tenant farming, or worse.

Beneath the Peasants came the Artisans; as a carpenter, Joseph, and his family, belonged to this class. Lower still were the Degraded and Expendable classes – the outcasts, beggars, outlaws, hustlers, laborers and slaves – maybe as much as ten percent of the population.

In most respects, the society Jesus lived in was one that few modern westerners would want to endure for very long, especially if they were not members of the ruling elite, or if they were women, children, slaves, or members of a subjugated ethnic group. For the general population, life in lower Galilee was all work and very little play, and often yielded little return or reward for labour.

Many of the people Jesus knew would have experienced lives of poverty, fear, suspicion, and anxiety. Crossan states that approximately 150,000 people were killed over a 30-year period in Israel between 67 and 37BC; fifty years later the situation had improved little. The reality of the occupying forces, the splintered factions in Jewish society – including collaborators and terrorists – the heavy tax burden, and economic hardships should cause us to rethink any romanticised, sanitised images we may have absorbed from childhood Sunday school lessons.

We turn now to a question that at some time many of us have wondered about, including, of course, artists and film directors: What did Jesus look like?

The face of Jesus has probably been painted and written about more than that of anyone else in history, so it might be thought that we would have some idea of his appearance. Despite thousands seeing Jesus during his lifetime, including 500 who were witnesses after his resurrection (1 Corinthians 15:6), the biblical accounts offer little clue as to what Jesus looked like. Paul seems decidedly disinterested: "From now on we regard no one from a worldly point of view. Though we once regarded Christ in this way, we do so no longer" *(2 Corinthians 5:16)*. This may have been for cultural and religious reasons – Jews were commanded not to make portraits or representations of God *(Exodus 20:4)*, or because it was of no importance – Jesus was an ordinary Jew with no distinctive features to mark him as different from others in his community. Although Jesus "tented among us" and we beheld his glory *(John 1:14)*, his glory is not about what he looked like. This was simply not a concern.

The Letter of Lentulus, assumed to be by a Roman official who had seen Jesus, describes him as "tall in stature and admirable" with "hair the colour of an unripe hazelnut and it falls smoothly to his ears." Unfortunately, the letter was later found to be written in the Middle Ages, and of no historical value.

For some, the Turin Shroud, the supposed burial cloth of Jesus, gives us an impression of how Jesus looked. While the Shroud's authenticity has been severely questioned by many, it remains (if genuine) the closest approximation we have to what Jesus might have looked like at the close of his life. In recent years, Italian detectives, accustomed to 'ageing' photographs of wanted gangsters to help track down the fugitives, have reversed this process in an attempt to envisage what the figure portrayed on the shroud looked like as a boy.

A different approach has come from insights derived from forensic anthropology and applied to skeletal remains of Jewish men alive in first century Israel. These have enabled British and Israeli scientists and artists to describe the appearance of Jesus more accurately than he is often depicted in Western art. Archaeologists inform us that the average height of a Jewish male was 5 ft 1in (155cm) and that he would have weighed about 110 pounds (50kg).

Expert in Christian origins, Professor Joan Taylor has extensively examined all the historical texts and skeletal records from Jerusalem to the time of Christ and concludes the commonly depicted image of Jesus as a white man would have been unrealistic for the region at the time. If we knew what Mary looked like, we might have seen a family likeness if he shared some of her features, but of course we do not.

Joan Taylor believes Jesus may have been taller and writes:

> Judaeans of this time were closest biologically to Iraqi Jews of the contemporary world. In terms of a color palette then, think dark-brown to black hair, deep brown eyes, olive-brown skin.

Jesus would have been a man of Middle Eastern appearance. In terms of height, an average man of this time stood 166 cm (5 ft 5ins) tall.[118]

Can we be any more specific though? Since Jesus' work as an adult was physically demanding he would probably have been quite fit and muscular. As a typical Galilean craftsman working outdoors, his face was probably weather-beaten. He would be slight and shaggily bearded since shaving was considered a luxury for the rich in the Middle East. Paul claims to have seen the Lord *(Acts 9:17)*, and also said that it was disgraceful for the men of Corinth to have long hair *(1 Corinthians 11:14)*. Perhaps Paul may not have written this if Jesus did have long hair (as the shroud of Turin depicts him)?

Did Jesus look older than his years? Possibly, for on one occasion we read that his accusers remarked, "You are not yet fifty years old" *(John 8:57)* – a strange remark about one twenty years younger. Life expectancy in Israel was low – between 35-45 years, so when Jesus began his ministry, at about 30 years of age, he would have been considered at the very least mature, and to some rather old to begin a preaching ministry. Some experts believe that 90% died before their mid-forties and very few, maybe as low as 3%, survived to the age of 60. In the first century 60% of live births usually died by their mid-teens.

Jesus' Jewishness would also have been reflected in his clothes. Being faithful to the Law, he would have worn the *tsîtsith* ("tassel", *Numbers 15:37-41; Matthew 9:20, 14:36; Luke 8:44*), and also perhaps the *tephillin* ("phylacteries", *Deuteronomy 6:8*), small boxes bound to arm and head containing the scriptural verses *Exodus 13:1-16, Deuteronomy 6:4-9* and *11:13-21*. By convention, these accessories were to be discreet; boxes on the arm, for example, invisible under clothing. A rabbinic source suggests that a box attached to the head should only be worn in winter beneath a headband, not in summer when it would have been conspicuous.

The truth is that none of the Gospel writers gives us clues of what Jesus looked like. The prophet Isaiah, referring to the Servant of the Lord, wrote that there was nothing exceptional about his appearance. "He had no beauty or majesty to attract us to him, nothing in his appearance that we should desire him" *(Isaiah 53:2)*. Centuries later New Testament

---

[118] Joan E. Taylor, *What did Jesus look like?*

writers would identify this passage of scripture with Jesus. There was nothing in his outward looks to cause others to stop and stare, to wonder about his heritage, question his roots, or think there was anything particularly remarkable about this man. Appearances can be so deceptive.

CHAPTER ELEVEN

The Parenting of God

> The wise evangelist, having shown us the Word made flesh, goes on to demonstrate that ... "he complied with the laws of the nature which he had made his own."
>
> *Cyril of Alexandria*

A mother's influence upon a very young child usually exceeds that of father, relatives, and all others. To understand the impact Mary had upon Jesus we have only to listen to the words she spoke after her cousin Elizabeth pronounced, "Blessed are you among women, and blessed is the child you bear" *(Luke 1:42)*. In the exultant song we know as the *Magnificat (Luke 1:46-55)*, Mary thanked God for righting all wrongs and choosing the powerless over the powerful. It is a song that reveals her humility, spiritual strength, and trust.

The joyful chorus echoes that of Hannah who, more than 1,000 years previously, had rejoiced in the birth of Samuel. Mary does this in a prophetic song full of allusions to a dozen different Old Testament prayers, including the books of Samuel, Isaiah, Habakkuk, Genesis, Job, and the Psalms. Apart from revealing an extraordinary degree of biblical literacy for someone who was likely still a teenager, Mary's words show a passion and understanding of God that must have been the fruit of her own godly upbringing *(cf. 2 Timothy 3:15 and 1:4-5)*.

Her prophetic words, "From now on all generations will call me blessed" *(Luke 1:48)*, were fulfilled initially in the respect and love shown by her husband Joseph – and by her son. We might also say that Jesus' world view was first spelled out in her words *(Luke 1:50-55)*.

> His mercy extends to those who fear him,
> from generation to generation.
> He has performed mighty deeds with his arm;
> he has scattered those who are proud in their inmost thoughts.
> He has brought down rulers from their thrones

but has lifted up the humble.
He has filled the hungry with good things
but has sent the rich away empty.
He has helped his servant Israel,
remembering to be merciful
to Abraham and his descendants forever,
just as he promised our ancestors.

The formation of Jesus' human psyche was profoundly influenced by the nurture of his mother. Mary's humility, wisdom and character, and submission to God, are revealed in her song. Now facing the greatest challenge in her young life, Mary would help shape Jesus' personality as he followed her example. He became like the obedient son described in the early chapters of Proverbs, who "[kept his] father's commands and [did] not forsake his mother's teaching" *(Proverbs 1:8, 6:20).* There is much of Mary in Jesus. Might Jesus' prayerfulness, for example, have been modelled on what he saw in his mother's life? Jack Dominian concludes:

> I see the childhood of Jesus as an interaction between Mary and Jesus in which Jesus developed his individuality, to which Mary responded by safeguarding its essentials. She did not only give birth to the baby, but her selection by God as a unique personality safeguarded her whole mothering from impeding the growth of Jesus.[119]

What other qualities of Mary do we see later in Jesus' life? Jesus was brought up in a home that seemed to show unusual respect for women. As his adult teaching reveals, his ease among women and his respect for them was revolutionary for his time. Jesus vigorously promoted the dignity and equality of women in the midst of a male-dominated society. At least to some degree he must have been taught this at home, observing the esteem shown by Joseph to his wife, an approval that came ultimately from God. This liberating honour and recognition afforded women by Jesus throughout his ministry was birthed perhaps with the angel's words to his mother, "Greetings, you who are highly favoured! The Lord is with you" *(Luke 1:28).*

---

[119] Jack Dominion, *One Like Us: A Psychological Interpretation of Jesus*

Mary's response to the angelic messenger on being told she would bear the Son of God captures an attitude of heart that was to reflect a lifetime of faithful obedience. "I am the Lord's servant. May your word to me be fulfilled" *(Luke 1:38)*. She shouldered more responsibilities than any other mother and is rightly admired by many for the way she discharged her duties. Mary's constancy is poignant. She endured what no mother should – though many do – the agonising death of a child; she chose to be with him until the end of his mortal life. Moreover, she was present at the birth of the church *(Acts 1:14)*.

How might the enormity and gravity of the challenge that lay before them have been for Joseph? While an angel had revealed to him the identity of his oldest child, there had been no instructions or precedent for what he was now called to do. How should he raise this child, not his natural son, yet he was given the role of his natural father – and this in the knowledge that Jesus was the Son of God? It is a staggering question Joseph must surely have asked.

No doubt this precipitated much discussion and prayer for Mary and Joseph, and not just in the early years. Perhaps Joseph might have found inspiration from the Genesis account of his namesake, the patriarch Joseph. Having been sold into slavery by his jealous brothers, Joseph rose to become the second most powerful man in the land where his presence and office resulted in Israel leaving Canaan at a time of famine and settling in Egypt. Jacob had succumbed to the temptation of favouritism by singling out Joseph for special attention over his brothers. This would have stood as a cautionary warning for Mary and Joseph, having glimpsed themselves the significance of what might lie ahead for their eldest son.

Jesus himself may well have gained wisdom from the Old Testament account of Joseph who, as teenager, boasted so freely of his dreams and future leadership to his brothers, stirring up their jealousy and hatred of him *(Genesis 37-50)*. We can assume that the young Jesus lacked Joseph's pride, was wiser than the patriarch, and said little or nothing to his siblings despite his growing awareness of his identity; we read of their later scepticism: "Even his brothers did not all believe in him" *(John 7:5)*.

Let us imagine Joseph recalling this Genesis story one day with Jesus...

"Son, put your tools down for a moment. Come and sit down; I've something I want to share with you. You're 17 now and your mother and I have known from the start that God has his hand on your life. He has great plans he wants to fulfil through you. And we know that you too sense this. I dare say that you know more about it than we do.

"Before you were born, Jesus, I had dreams about you. So many times I wanted to tell others that God has plans for you. It would have been so easy to speak of you as my special son. But I followed your mother's example. She spoke little of all the things she had been shown; instead she treasured them in her heart.

"My own parents named me after Jacob's son, our forefather Joseph, who brought deliverance to our people. He started out as a shepherd boy, not all that far from here. From early on, he would have looked after sheep on these hillsides. But life wasn't easy; his parents weren't always wise and his brothers didn't understand him – in fact, they rather resented him. They could see he was the favoured son and they became jealous. Now think of your brothers, James, Joses, Judas, Simon. They're good lads, but they're already noticing that you're not like them. The way you talk about God, the way you read the scriptures – even the way you stay out of trouble. They know you are different – well, special. I can understand how they feel. Don't take it badly if they tease you or try to make you do something wrong. Your mother and I try to stop them, but we're not always around. One day they'll understand and appreciate what God is doing through you; but it may take a while.

"When Joseph was your age – just 17 – God was with him and gave him powerful dreams about what lay ahead. Dreams about how he would rise to prominence and even how his family would bow before him to honour and acknowledge his status. With youthful zeal, but not a lot of wisdom, he spoke of these dreams and what they meant, telling his brothers how God would set him above them all one day. And, as you know, it did indeed come to pass, but before this there were many obstacles and setbacks. It wasn't till he was 30 that he rose to a position of real influence.

"Jesus, don't be unwise and share what God has for you before the time is right. You would be misunderstood and it would be harder for you. I wouldn't be surprised if you weren't 30 by the time people are looking to you for leadership and guidance – and, who knows, how our nation can be saved. Take some time to meditate on Joseph's story in Genesis, Jesus. I'm sure the Father will show you many things."

For someone who played such a significant role in the Genesis account, it is perhaps surprising that the patriarch Joseph is only mentioned twice in the New Testament. Christians have often drawn parallels to illustrate how he foreshadows Jesus. But were some of these similarities first identified by Jesus – and his father? Did this awareness go on to shape Jesus' attitudes and guide his behaviour? Of course, we cannot be sure. Yet when references to Joseph in Genesis are set alongside those from the New Testament some parallels can be noticed.

Joseph	*Parallels*	*Jesus*
37:3	His father loved him dearly	Matthew 3:17
37:2	A shepherd of his father's sheep	John 10:11,27-29
37:13,14	Sent by father to brothers	Hebrews 2:11
37:4	Hated by brothers without good reason	John 7:4-5
37:20	Others plotted to harm him	John 11:53
39:7	Resisted difficult temptations	Matthew 4:1
37:26	Taken to Egypt to avoid being killed	Matthew 2:14-15
37:23	Robes taken from him	John 19:23, 24
37:28	Sold for the price of a slave	Matthew 26:15
39:20	Bound in chains	Matthew 27:2
39:16-18	Falsely accused	Matthew 26:59-60
39:20	Remained silent and offered no defence	Isaiah 53:7
39:21	Respected by his jailer	Luke 23:47
40:2-3	Placed with two prisoners: one saved, one lost	Luke 23:32
41:38	Filled with the Spirit of God	Luke 4:1
41:46	Aged 30 at the start of public recognition	Luke 3:23
41:57	Gave bread to hungry people	John 6:48-58
41:41	Exalted after suffering	Philippians 2:9-11
41:45	Took non-Jewish brides (the Church)	Ephesians 3:1-12
42:8	Not recognised by own brethren	Luke 24:37

Joseph	Parallels	Jesus
45:1-15	Forgave those who wronged him	Luke 23:34
45:1-15	Restored repentant brothers	Zechariah 12:10
45:7	Saved the nation	Matthew 1:21
45:7-8	Humble and unspoiled by wealth	John 13:12
41:57	Visited and honoured by all earthly nations	Isaiah 2:2,3, 49:6
50:20	What others did to hurt, God turned to good	1 Corinthians 2:7

Joseph's relationship as a father to Jesus would have changed over time – as it does with any parent and child. In order to probe deeper, devotional writer Max Lucado devised a host of questions he would like to have asked Jesus' parents, ranging from the frivolous (Did they ever arm-wrestle – if so, who won?) to the inspiring (Did Joseph ever look up from his prayers and see Jesus listening?) We cannot be sure of the answers, but our responses may provide us with a litmus test of our own attitude towards this paradox about Jesus' human and divine natures. Do we unwittingly allow a 'super-saintly' image of Jesus to cloud our appreciation of his humanity – as one of us? Here are some of Lucado's questions:

> Joseph, how did Jesus respond when he saw other children giggling during the service at the synagogue? When he saw a rainbow, did he ever mention a flood? Did you ever feel awkward teaching him how he created the world? When he saw a lamb being led to the slaughter, did he act differently? Did you ever see him with a distant look on his face as if he were listening to someone you couldn't hear? How did he act at funerals? Did you ever try to count the stars with him and succeed? Did Jesus ever come home with a black eye? How did he act when he got his first haircut? Did he have any friends by the name of Judas? Did Jesus do well in school? Did you ever scold him? Did he ever have to ask a question about scripture? What do you think he thought when he saw a prostitute offering to the highest bidder the body he made? Did he ever get angry when someone was dishonest with him? Did you ever catch him pensively looking at the flesh on his own arm while holding a clod of dirt? Did he ever wake up

afraid? Who was his best friend? When someone referred to Satan, how did he act? Did you accidentally call him Father? What did he and his cousin John talk about as kids?[120]

Some questions are profound, others appear banal – possibly offensive to some. Nevertheless, they challenge us to reflect on matters often overlooked. Significantly, the Gospel records are silent about such things, and to proceed too far down this line of speculation is to repeat the error of later apocryphal writings, such as the *Infancy Gospel of Thomas*, which go beyond the borders of the biblical portrait. It was because many early Christians found it difficult to accept the silence of the New Testament concerning Jesus' formative years that they created stories to fill the gaps. The majority of scholars recognise these for what they are – contrived tales, far removed from historical reality.

---

[120] Max Lucado, *God Came Near*, 25

CHAPTER TWELVE

A Down-to-Earth Jesus

There is much to fathom in Christ, for he is like an abundant mine with many recesses of treasures, so that however deep men go they never reach the end ... but rather in every recess find new veins with new riches everywhere.

St John of the Cross

Since the children have flesh and blood, he [Jesus Christ] too shared in their humanity so that by his death he might destroy him who holds the power of death – that is, the devil – and free those who all their lives were held in slavery by their fear of death. For surely it is not angels he helps, but Abraham's descendants. For this reason, he had to be made like his brothers in every way, in order that he might become a merciful and faithful high priest in service to God, and that he might make atonement for the sins of the people. Because he himself suffered when he was tempted, he is able to help those who are being tempted.

Hebrews 2:14-17

And in this skin, I live and sweat and breathe and groan. My shoulders ache. My eyes are dry from these dreadful rainless days – from the long walks to Sepphoris through the grey fields in which the seeds burn under the dim winter sun because the rains don't come...[121]

Anne Rice

Living under the Roman occupation in Israel and the heavy tax burden the military government imposed, most people in Jesus' time were concerned for their own survival rather than the luxuries of life. In

---

[121] Anne Rice, *Christ the Lord, the Road to Cana,* 4

describing the plight of the citizens, it is not hard to imagine the burden on an ordinary family. Kirk Kimball writes:

> In addition to the Roman income tax, there are many other new taxes – on land, crops, cattle, and for tribute to Rome's "divine" emperor, Tiberius Caesar. There is even a tax on all boys over 14 and all girls over 12. Not to mention bridge and harbor tolls, town dues, and various other fees. All together these taxes take up to 40% of a Hebrew man's total yearly output. This is a near-impossible burden for families barely subsisting on already meagre incomes.

Despite the fertility of Galilee, this financial pressure resulted in many being forced into losing their own land and becoming tenant farmers, as John Pilch outlines:

> Peasants from the Judean countryside were deeply in debt. In first century Palestine as much as 35-40% of total agricultural production was eaten up by a variety of taxes. Peasants unable to pay lost ownership of the land and became sharecroppers. As demands on them became even greater, many fled the land. Many became artisans. Thus artisans and non-elites from Jerusalem were not much better off than the peasants.[122]

Joseph and Mary's social status is clearly indicated when they went to the Temple to offer purification rites shortly after Jesus' birth. Like many other families with neither the ability to purchase a lamb nor the land on which to raise one, they could offer instead the less expensive sacrifice of two doves, in obedience to *Leviticus 12:1-8.* E. P. Sanders vividly describes the typical lifestyles of many residents in the area:

> The farm-dwelling peasants in Galilee worked six days a week from dawn to dusk, and on the Sabbath they rested. They had neither the money nor the time to jaunt into a nearby city for the afternoon drama. They may have gone to the city to sell their goods in the market, but, afterwards, they seldom had the money to stay overnight and participate in cultural events. Nor did they have the money to take weekend trips to Tyre and Sidon, where there were even greater Hellenistic treats.

---

[122] Pilch, J. C., *The Cultural World of Jesus*

Even if they had the money, they would have transgressed the Sabbath by travelling, and very few of them did that.

Galilean villages specialised in different trades. Although a relatively unimportant village in southern Galilee, Nazareth was known for its carpenters; archaeological evidence supports the manufacture of furniture in the area at that time. Joseph's workshop could then have been one of a number of craftsmen's shops in the town centre.

According to tradition, a chief duty of a father, irrespective of social status, was to ensure that his sons learned a useful trade, one handed down through the generations. "Just as it is necessary to feed one's son, so it is necessary to teach him a manual trade," stated the Talmud. Joseph therefore had an obligation to make Jesus his apprentice; indeed, as the rabbis taught, "He who works for a living is greater than he who shuts himself up in idle piety." In the case of siblings, the younger boys could learn by watching their older brothers. As Joseph passed on the family business to Jesus, so we can picture James, the next son, being trained in the carpentry trade as well.

Assuming Jesus, like many contemporaries, finished his formal schooling at 13, he may have joined his father in the business then, having been trained in the craft from an early age. This would have been not long after the family's trip to Jerusalem recorded in the Gospels.

Tradesmen were instantly recognizable by the symbols they wore: carpenters put wood chips behind their ears, tailors stuck needles in their tunics, and dyers wore coloured rags. Interestingly, on the Sabbath these badges were left at home, perhaps to recognise that all were equal before God. Woodworking was viewed as a clean trade – unlike, for example, tanning hides which involved touching animal carcasses and becoming ritually unclean. Carpentry required intelligence, training, dexterity, concentration, and physical energy; carpenters of that time would work with a variety of tools: axes for felling trees, an adze for shaping wood, hatchets, iron saws, bow drills, stone-headed hammers, wooden mallets, iron chisels, files, awls, and planes. For measuring they used a rule, compass, and dividers; chalk and pencil were used to score patterns and guide cutting. Joseph and Jesus would have crafted with local wood: sycamore, olive, and possibly oak. They would have made wooden carts, ploughs, winnowing forks and yokes for local farmers, and posts, beams, doors, and doorframes for house construction. For indoors, tables, chairs, and wooden boxes were common items required.

What might Jesus' own family home have been like? Nick Page describes typical accommodation:

> The homes of ordinary poor families of the time were frequently built on two levels: there was the lower level where the everyday living took place, and an upper mezzanine where the family slept. Or, if they were caves (and many people did live in caves at the time) the families would have slept in the central parts and to the back, with the animals kept at the entrance. Israel can get very cold at night, so the animals would have been a heating source for the house: a kind of primitive central heating system.[123]

Justin Martyr (c.100-165) says in his *Dialogue with Trypho* that Jesus made yokes and ploughs. The word translated "carpenter" in the Gospels (Greek: *tekton*), is in fact broader in meaning than just one who works in wood. It denotes someone more like a general construction worker, able to work with many materials. It is likely therefore that the "carpenter's son" *(Matthew 13:55; Mark 6:3)* would also have worked in stone, metal, and brick.[124] Wood was a scarce commodity in Israel, especially so in the part of Galilee where Jesus lived. Hence most houses were built of stone or dug into the sides of hills. A *tekton* would therefore have been required to turn his hand to a number of crafts, including some masonry and basic metal work.

Let us consider how the training Jesus received at his father's side might have influenced his broader learning and later informed his own teaching. His relationship with Joseph in some respects reflected his relationship with his heavenly Father. Jesus the apprentice listened to his earthly father and was trained for a practical trade. Jesus the disciple listened to his heavenly Father and was trained for his teaching ministry.

Jesus experienced the kindness of a generous and loving father training his son. This may have prompted remarks such as those recorded in *Matthew 11:27* and those about the man who gives good gifts to his son *(Matthew 5:9-11)*. In Joseph's love of Jesus, we can imagine that Jesus identified with his earthly father and took after him. He was born

---

[123] Nick Page, *What Happened to the Ark of the Covenant and other Bible Mysteries*, 80-81

[124] According to a second-century tradition, Jesus made ploughs, yokes, and other farm equipment.

in a patriarchal society where the father was of considerable importance and the relationship between father and son of paramount significance.

The intimacy and warmth with which Jesus describes his relationship with his heavenly Father could not have come about if he had not experienced something similar with his earthly father. This interpretation lends itself to the common-sense view, often psychologically validated, that the child is the father of the man. I simply cannot visualise the closeness of Jesus with Yahweh if he had not first experienced something similar on earth.

This is the pattern John sets out:

> The Son can do nothing of his own accord, but only what he sees the Father doing. For the Father loves the Son and shows him all that he is himself doing.
>
> *John 5:19-20*

Not only did Jesus trust the Father, he also honoured him *(John 5:23)*. "I seek not to do my own will, but the will of him who sent me." *(John 5:30)*. Work for Jesus was a duty and a sacrament. He took the form of a servant rather than a master *(Philippians 2:7)*.

Jesus' upbringing in a small Galilean town and his practical skills would have brought him into contact with many aspects of everyday village and country life, later to be used in his teaching ministry. In Luke's Gospel we see that Jesus highlights the need for careful planning before building *(14:28-30)*; he later speaks of "a stone rejected by builders that became the keystone" *(Luke 20:17)*, alluding to *Psalm 118:22*.

An event that undoubtedly had a profound effect upon Jesus was the death of Joseph. When this was can only be surmised. If Joseph married Mary in his early twenties, he may have died in his forties which in those days was considered elderly, leaving Jesus with responsibilities as head of the household. From the cross Jesus would entrust his mother Mary into John's safekeeping *(John 19:26-27)*, which only makes sense if Joseph was dead by then.

That Joseph is not mentioned either at the start of Jesus' public ministry, the wedding in Cana *(John 2:1-11)*, or when Jesus returned to Nazareth shortly after *(Mark 6:1-6)*, suggests that he had died by that time. However, on one occasion during his ministry, when Mary and his siblings came to see him, Jesus taught, "Whoever does the will of God is my mother and brothers and sisters" *(Mark 3:31-35)*. Could it have been to tell him of his father's death that his family had come?

We have little idea how long Jesus had had these additional responsibilities as the new head of the family. By the time of his preaching in Capernaum, the family had relocated there from Nazareth. Here the people had said of him:

> Isn't this the carpenter's son? Is not his mother called Mary? And are not his brothers James and Joseph and Simon and Judas? And are not all his sisters with us?
>
> *Matthew 13:55*

"Isn't this the carpenter's son?" This simple statement alone discredits all the fanciful theories about where Jesus spent the 'hidden years' of his life. This is how he was known locally; there is no mention of him living elsewhere or having any occupation other than following in his father's footsteps. If he was still working as a carpenter when Joseph died, he would have faced bereavement in the family, and the added necessity to provide for them. He had to handle the tensions, misunderstandings, pressures, and joys of family life. In all this, God was causing all things to work together for the good of the Son he loved *(Romans 8:28)*. The Father was Lord of his circumstances, quietly training him and ensuring that, in the ordinary and mundane, Jesus "had to be made like his brothers in every respect" *(Hebrews 2:17, ESV)*. "He had to be made like them, fully human in every way…"

Jesus may have had to oversee the marriage arrangements for his sisters among his other duties. These practical reasons may in part be why Jesus did not begin his ministry sooner. As the eldest, he would have shouldered the main responsibility to provide for his family through his practical skills. Jesus may well have delayed entering into public life until James, the next brother, was sufficiently mature to take over the responsibilities left by their father's absence. It is also possible, of course, that the four younger brothers moved out of the area in search of employment.

The writer to the Hebrews confirms the authenticity of Jesus' human experience and uses that as a stepping stone to validate our own, and Jesus' support for us. Jesus had "flesh and blood", so too do we. He had to be made like his brothers (and sisters) "in all things" *(Hebrews 2:17, NASB)*; this statement is breathtaking in its extensiveness. He was tempted as we are and suffered as we do. He experienced the same breadth of emotions: compassion and love, indignation and annoyance, joy and sorrow. Because he has experienced life as we do, he is in a position to help us – particularly in times of difficulty and testing. How far this is from the way Jesus is sometimes portrayed in films – remote and robbed of humanity and, therefore, of little use to us.

The biblical portrait is of one who is intensely practical, who encounters the same problems as his peers and therefore has empathy and understanding of the human condition. There is an earthy realism about him, reflected in the everyday, the trivial, the mundane. He knew, for example, the problem of getting a speck of sawdust in the eye *(Matthew 7:3-5)*, the wisdom of building a foundation on rock rather than on sand *(7:24-27)*. He knew too of the destructive action of moths and rust *(6:19-20)*, sewing patches on cloth, pouring wine into wineskins *(9:16-17)*, and using storerooms in a house *(13:52)*. He spoke of farming and farmers, sackcloth and ashes, yokes, pearls, millstones, a watchtower, and tombs. Jesus knew about the need for oil in oil lamps *(5:15, 25:3-4,8-10)*, the value of coins *(20:2,9-10,13, 22:19-21)*, the function of a capstone *(21:42,44)*, paying taxes *(22:15-21)*, and the use of flat roofs on houses *(24:17)*. He referred to everyday kitchen items including salt, yeast, flour, bread, spices, and the washing of dishes.

Jesus was an accurate observer of nature, speaking with familiarity about birds, vultures, dogs, pigs, wolves, sheep, snakes, doves, fish, gnats, camels, hens and chicks, goats, lilies, grass, trees with good and bad fruit, thorn bushes and thistles, figs and fig trees, reeds, seeds, weeds, wheat, mustard seed, harvesting, and grapes and vineyards. Indeed, his childhood training, schooling, and observations of life around him contributed strongly to the vivid and colourful teaching he would later give.

While Jesus grew up in a society more akin to one in the developing world today rather than the contemporary Western style, there are nevertheless elements that are common to us all. He faced similar pressures and temptations that confront people in every generation and society. Like each of us, he too lived in the midst of circumstances that at times seemed to obscure the reality of God's presence, power or love. Growing up in a time when violence was commonplace and in a climate of suspicion and hostility, his parents and family must often have experienced anxiety and fear. For years he witnessed the anguish of seeing cruelty, suffering, poverty, and injustice without recourse to actively change things, knowing it was not yet "his time".

At a family level, he experienced the gamut of emotions of normal life – including the grief of loss and bereavement: his father Joseph, probably aunts, uncles, and children dying in infancy. However close his parents were to him, there was no one with whom he could really share his heart. As he emerged from his teenage years, there would have been social pressure for him to get married, settle down, and start a family. In hard economic times, he experienced the financial pressures of running a small business. He knew about the need to work hard and long to provide for his family. In his personal relationships, he would have known the heartache of being misunderstood by family members – and later as he embarked on a mission that he knew would cause them pain, perplexity, and loss. He had to live with emotional tensions, even some of his own relatives doubting him. He truly shared in the human condition and in so doing is an inspiration and example to all of us.

God in Jesus loved us to the point of subjecting himself to our most mundane as well as our most agonising experiences. As the God-Man he suffered intensely; he did not pass unscathed through the trauma of Gethsemane and Calvary. Far from it; because he was God, he endured suffering that was in full proportion to the depth of his love and the greatness of his person.

Eminent 19th century Jewish scholar Alfred Edersheim concludes his survey of Jesus' background with these words:

> Among such a people, and in that country, Jesus spent by far the longest part of his life upon earth. Generally, this period may be described as that of his true and full human development – physical, intellectual, spiritual – of outward submission to man and inward submission to God, with the attendant results of "wisdom," "favor," and "grace".[125]

---

[125] Edersheim, A., *The Life and Times of Jesus the Messiah* (Hendrickson, Peabody, Massachusetts, 1883)

Chapter Thirteen

Fisherman, Prophet, and Messiah

Rabbi Yeshua ben Yoseph. Who did Jesus think he was? He showed no indication of suffering an identity crisis, no need to engage in the tiresome modern hobby of finding oneself. He apparently was quite sure of who he was, though no one since has been ... The crux of the problem lies in the paradox that, although Jesus rarely spoke directly about his own status, he implicitly made himself the pivotal figure in the final drama he was announcing and inaugurating.

James Charlesworth

In the beginning was the Word, and the Word was with God, and the Word was God. He was with God in the beginning. Through him all things were made; without him nothing was made that has been made. In him was life, and that life was the light of all mankind. The light shines in the darkness, and the darkness has not overcome it.

John 1:1-5

In this chapter, we consider two relatives who in their distinctive ways became powerful advocates for Jesus: John the fisherman and Gospel writer, and John the prophet. We further reflect on how Jesus viewed himself and how his convictions influenced these two family members.

By carefully collating information from the Gospel accounts it is possible to trace genealogies for Salome and Mary. Concerning the calling of the first disciples, we read, "Going on from there, [Jesus] saw two other brothers, James son of Zebedee and his brother John. They were in a boat with their father Zebedee" *(Matthew 4:21).* The Gospel writers noted the onlookers at the crucifixion: "Among them were Mary Magdalene, Mary the mother of James and Joseph, and the mother of Zebedee's sons" *(Matthew 27:56).* "Near the cross of Jesus stood his mother, his mother's sister, Mary the wife of Clopas, and Mary

Magdalene" *(John 19:25)*. "Some women were watching from a distance. Among them were Mary Magdalene, Mary the mother of James the younger and of Joseph, and Salome" *(Mark 15:40)*.

Most commentators suggest that in all probability Salome was John's mother, Mary's sister and therefore Jesus' aunt. John was therefore not only one of Jesus' best friends but also a close relative – his first cousin. Capernaum, where Zebedee's fishing business was based, became the home of Jesus and his family when they moved from Nazareth to live near Lake Galilee. This would indicate that Jesus knew his aunt Salome well and may explain the title for John in his Gospel as "the disciple whom Jesus loved". Since Jewish family ties were strong, it is easy to imagine they may have grown up together in Galilee and travelled together as pilgrims to the annual festivals in Jerusalem.

They may have been close friends long before Jesus called John and his brother James, sons of Zebedee, to leave their nets and follow him *(Mark 1:19-20)*. How often did they play together as children, talk about their work, family life, and most importantly, the faith they held dear? Certainly, John's response to Jesus' call was immediate and wholehearted when he left the family fishing business to become a disciple *(Matthew 4:21-22)*. There is no hint of any hesitation or doubt that he was doing the right thing. It seems that John was simply responding intuitively to all he had come to appreciate about his cousin over the years.

John, Jesus' closest disciple, opens his Gospel with breathtaking statements about Jesus' identity and mission *(John 1:1-18)*. "The true light that gives light to everyone was coming into the world" *(John 1:9)*. This humble carpenter is the *Logos*, the Word made flesh, the ultimate representation and revelation of God. These are remarkable pronouncements. At what point on John's own journey of faith did he reach such convictions? These full revelations perhaps came only after he received the gift of the Spirit – when the resurrected Jesus breathed his Spirit upon him *(John 20:22)*.

For Jesus, these insights had developed years earlier. Some hold that it was not until he began his public ministry that Jesus fully appreciated who he was and why he had come to earth. As we have sought to demonstrate though, it seems more likely that his self-awareness came gradually during the preceding three decades of his life. Although there might have been significant crises in his youth and early manhood that furthered his understanding, for the most part it was something that grew from his earliest childhood, coming to maturity before he left the family home in Nazareth for the journey south to be baptised.

Another close relative of Jesus, also a cousin, was John 'the baptiser' – *Yohanan* 'the immerser'. Their first 'meeting' could not have been more dramatic *(Luke 1:41-43)*. Their mothers, Elizabeth and Mary, shared the experience of a miraculous conception of a son prophesied about before birth. It is likely that the two families would have met often over the years; they had much to talk about.

Just as Joseph and Mary shared with Jesus the events surrounding his birth, so we can imagine Zechariah and Elizabeth doing the same with their son. John and Jesus would have learned of each other's calling and destiny in God. Indeed, Jesus might even have begun to take a lead in guiding John to a deeper knowledge and experience of his role and purpose. Before John was old enough to understand, Zechariah had prophesied over him:

> And you, my child, will be called a prophet of the Most High;
> for you will go on before the Lord to prepare the way for him,
> to give his people the knowledge of salvation through the
> forgiveness of their sins.

Luke 1:76-77

These words recalled Malachi's prophecy of God's messenger:

> "I will send my messenger, who will prepare the way before
> me. Then suddenly the Lord you are seeking will come to his
> Temple; the messenger of the covenant, whom you desire, will
> come," says the Lord Almighty.

Malachi 3:1

Together with the words of Isaiah, this would prove pivotal in John's understanding of his own ministry; to "prepare the way of the Lord" *(Isaiah 40:3)*, for "the glory of the Lord will be revealed and all people will see it together" *(40:5)*; "the Sovereign Lord comes with power" *(40:10)* and "He tends his flock like a shepherd" *(40:11)*.

We have seen the profound effect Isaiah's prophecy also had upon Jesus' own understanding. Perhaps it was Jesus who first introduced the significance of Isaiah's prophecies to John, encouraging him to see how relevant these were to both of them. We know that John understood his own purpose in coming "to make straight the way for the Lord" *(John 1:23)*. Of Jesus, he proclaimed:

"This is the one I meant when I said, 'A man who comes after me has surpassed me because he was before me.' I myself did not know ["recognize", NASB] him, but the reason I came baptizing with water was that he might be revealed to Israel..."

Then John gave this testimony: "I saw the Spirit come down from heaven as a dove and remain on him ... The one who sent me to baptize with water told me, "The man on whom you see the Spirit come down and remain is the one who will baptize with the Holy Spirit."

John 1:30-33

The implication of the New American Standard Bible (NASB), quoted here in brackets, is, "I did not recognise Jesus as the Messiah." Alternatively, it is possible that John did not recognise Jesus physically because they had not met for a few years. But the former seems more likely in light of a previous statement where John is unequivocal:

The next day John saw Jesus coming toward him and said, "Look, the Lamb of God, who takes away the sin of the world."

John 1:29

We may wonder to what extent, at that time, John realised the implications of his remarkable declaration.

One commonly held view is that during his long weeks in prison, John grew weak in faith. "When John, while imprisoned, heard of the works of Christ, he sent word by his disciples and said to him, 'Are you the Expected One, or shall we look for someone else?'" *(Matthew 11:3)* Did he now doubt the identity of the one he had recognised as the Messiah? Or was he in fact pursuing his goal to "make straight the way of the Lord"? It could be that by causing his disciples to go back to question Jesus, John was living out his objective, that "he [Jesus] must increase, but I must decrease" *(John 3:30)*. This would be the best way to shift the focus of his followers towards Jesus, knowing that they would readily embrace his cousin's leadership when he himself was gone. In this case, John's instructions can be seen as a signpost to Jesus of his faith, not a sign that he lacked it. Jesus responded with words from Isaiah (a favoured prophet of John) announcing miracles the Messiah would perform *(Matthew 11:4-6; cf. Isaiah 35:5f.)*. John's disciples would now know for certain that Jesus was indeed the Expected One and that they need look no further.

Both John the disciple and John the baptiser held a special place in Jesus' estimation. He described his cousin who lived in the desert as "one who is more than a prophet" *(Matthew 11:9)* and added "among those born of women there has not risen anyone greater than John the Baptist" *(Matthew 11:11)*, a unique affirmation from Jesus for this remarkably perceptive, courageous, and fearless man of God.

John, the fisherman and Gospel writer, alludes to "the disciple whom Jesus loved" *(John 13:23, 19:26, 20:2, 21:7,20)*. Rather than interpreting this as a boastful assertion of John's own ranking with Jesus, this can be seen as a literary device to conceal this disciple's identity. Nonetheless it indicates the depth of John's friendship and intimacy with his Lord. Jesus may indeed have felt closer to these two men – the prophet and the fisherman – than to anyone else. They were related, of similar age, and (most importantly) shared a profound passion for God and his purposes. How fascinating it would have been to eavesdrop on their conversations and observe their interactions.

As Jesus was being prepared for his ministry, the other two were also being prepared for their roles in the drama of redemption; John, the desert prophet, who would be Jesus' loyal herald, the forerunner preparing people for his coming, and John the fisherman – Jesus' companion and friend, and writer of the fourth Gospel. The two Johns were being prepared, to borrow Eugene Peterson's phrase, for "a long obedience in the same direction" and Jesus may well have had a mentoring role in their lives under the Father's watchful eye.

Jesus could only be their mentor if he was first crystal clear about his own identity. Let us probe a little deeper and see what factors might have influenced Jesus' own thinking. To understand the path he took, it is important to grasp an appreciation of his fellow Jews' beliefs and how he engaged with these.

According to leading theologian Tom Wright, in response to the question, *"Who are we?"* Jesus' contemporaries would respond, "We are Israel, the chosen people of the creator God". Their reply to, *"Where are we?"* was, "We are in the Holy Land," but, paradoxically, "We are also still in exile." To *"What is wrong?"* they would maintain, "We have the wrong rulers" – referring to pagans on the one hand (their Roman oppressors), compromised Jews on the other (as those who served the Romans' agenda), or something between (as with Herod and his family).

To *"What is the solution?"* they would reply, "Our God must act again to give us the right sort of rule," that is, his own kingship exercised through properly appointed officials (a true priesthood, possibly a true king). In the meantime, Israel must be faithful to God's covenant charter.

Wright maintains that Jesus understood himself as the one through whom God was fulfilling his promises to Israel; one functioning as a prophet, as Israel's messiah, and as the embodiment of Yahweh. His vocation was to be Israel-in-person, Israel's representative, and the one in whom Israel's destiny would reach its climax. He believed he was the Messiah.

> The difference between the beliefs of Jesus and those of thousands of other Jews of his day amounted simply to this: he believed, also, that all these things were coming true in and through himself.[126]

Jesus radically reframed Jewish faith and identity as it was then understood. God's kingdom was precisely about replacing the Temple system with the renewed heart which, itself celebrating the forgiveness of God, would love God and neighbour in the way that the *Shema*, the daily prayer of the Jews to this day, indicated as the heart of Jewish practice. Jesus was claiming to offer all that the Temple stood for.

Having established the broad contours of where Jesus stood in relation to his contemporaries, we can now examine Wright's perspective on Jesus' self-understanding.

> I do not think that Jesus "knew he was God" in the same sense that one knows he is tired or happy, male or female. He did not sit back and say to himself, "Well, I never! I'm the second person of the Trinity!" Rather "as part of his human vocation, grasped in faith, sustained in prayer, tested in confirmation, agonized over in further prayer and doubt, and implemented in action, he believed he had to do and be, for Israel and the world, that which according to scripture only YHWH himself could do and be".
>
> Let me be clear, also, what I am not saying. I do not think Jesus "knew he was God" in the same sense that one knows one is hungry or thirsty, tall or short. It was not a

---

126 Wright, *Jesus and the Victory of God,* 652

mathematical knowledge, like knowing that two and two make four; nor was it straightforwardly observational knowledge, like knowing that there is a bird on the fence outside my room because I can see and hear it. It was more like the knowledge that I have that I am loved by my family and closest friends; like the knowledge that I have that sunrise over the sea is awesome and beautiful; like the knowledge of the musician not only of what the composer intended but of how precisely to perform the piece in exactly that way – a knowledge most securely possessed, of course, when the performer is also the composer. It was, in short, the knowledge that characterizes vocation.

I suggest, in short, that the return of YHWH to Zion, and the Temple-theology which it brings into focus, are the deepest keys and clues to gospel Christology. Forget the "titles" of Jesus, at least for a moment; forget the pseudo-orthodox attempts to make Jesus conscious of being the second person of the Trinity; forget the arid reductionism that is the mirror-image of that unthinking would-be orthodoxy. Focus, instead, on a young Jewish prophet telling a story about YHWH returning to Zion as judge and redeemer, and then embodying it by riding into the city in tears, symbolizing the Temple's destruction and celebrating the final exodus. I propose, as a matter of history, that Jesus of Nazareth was conscious of a vocation: a vocation given him by the one he knew as "father", to enact himself what, in Israel's scriptures, God had promised to accomplish all by himself. He would be the pillar of cloud and fire for the people of the new exodus. He would embody in himself the returning and redeeming action of the covenant God.[127]

Wright's approach leads to a safe supposition that Jesus' self-awareness and sense of vocation were fashioned over an extended period of reflection prior to his ministry. Through his interactions with others, such as John the fisherman and John the prophet, his experience of synagogue and Temple, his meditation on the scriptures, and intimations from the Spirit, a clear understanding of his identity, calling, and destiny

---

[127] Wright, *Jesus and the Victory of God,* 629

emerged which he would then spend the next 1,000 days revealing to others.

Chapter Fourteen

Marriage Made in Heaven

> This is a profound mystery – but I am talking about Christ
> and the church.
>
> *Ephesians 5:32*

By the time Jesus was 30, most, if not all, his contemporaries in Nazareth
would have been married with children. In all likelihood Jesus had
attended many weddings – including those of family members – before
the one at Cana described in the Gospels *(John 2:1-12)*. In a patriarchal
society such as this, marriages were usually arranged by the fathers of the
two families involved. Marriage was seen as a transaction to secure the
future of a family through an alliance with another; it formed the basis
for a strong and close-knit community.

Marriage was understood to be an obligation, not an option; girls
could be betrothed as young as thirteen, and boys by their later teens.
The formalising of wedlock would then generally be entered into at an
early age by present-day standards. Life expectancy for men was around
35-45 at that time and Jewish men were often married by eighteen, Jewish
girls in their early to mid-teens. Rabbi Samuel the Younger, who lived
towards the close of the first century, taught that at eighteen a man was
"fit for the bridal chamber".[128]

> He who has no wife dwells without good, without help,
> without joy, without blessing, and without atonement.

This was a common sentiment among the rabbis.[129] Celibacy was rare
among Jews because they took the obligation to propagate the children
of Abraham very seriously. For someone to remain unmarried was not
unknown but was sufficiently unusual as to provoke comment. It was
thought wise to "marry off" young people early so as to limit the

---

[128] *Mishnah, Pirke Aboth 5.21*
[129] *Genesis Rabba 17:2*

possibility of sexual adventures, as the apocryphal book of Ecclesiasticus explains:

> A daughter is a secret anxiety to her father, and worry over her robs him of sleep; when she is young, for fear she may not marry, or if married, for fear she may be disliked; while a virgin, for fear she may be seduced and become pregnant in her father's house; or having a husband, for fear she may go astray, or, though married, for fear she may be barren.
>
> *Ecclesiasticus 42:9-10*

In his own community and neighbouring villages, Jesus would have witnessed family members, friends, and neighbours get married. In the decade before he began his ministry, as head of the family he may have been responsible for arranging marriages for his younger siblings – if, as seems likely, Joseph had died some years previously.

Had Jesus contemplated marriage for himself? No doubt others had considered marital options for Jesus, and perhaps wondered what was wrong with him that he appeared to show no interest. A key question we too face then is: Why did Jesus not marry? In more recent times, some have questioned Jesus' sexual orientation, while others have suggested possible partners, but there is no evidence for any of this. Committed, from perhaps his teenage years as we have suggested, to the fact that his own sacrificial death lay ahead, Jesus would have realised the anguish his mother would go through – "a sword will pierce your own soul" *(Luke 2:35)*. We can suppose too that, having observed the grief and difficulties for a wife at the loss of a husband and father to their children, Jesus may have considered the effect of this upon any wife of his own. Such considerations are valid, but the solution to our quest lies elsewhere.

Perhaps some answers lie in a discussion Jesus had with his followers. When questioned about divorce, Jesus, quoting from the Old Testament, replied that at the beginning the Creator made them male and female *(Genesis 1:27)*. He then said:

> For this reason, a man will leave his father and mother and be united to his wife, and the two will become one flesh. So they are no longer two, but one flesh. Therefore, what God has joined together, let no one separate ... Moses permitted you to divorce your wives because your hearts were hard. But it was not this way from the beginning. I tell you that anyone

who divorces his wife, except for sexual immorality, and marries another woman commits adultery.

Matthew 19:5-9

The disciples pressed him on this: "If this is the situation between a husband and wife, it is better not to marry" *(19:10)*, to which Jesus replied,

> Not everyone can accept this word, but only those to whom it has been given. For there are eunuchs who were born that way, and there are eunuchs who have been made eunuchs by others – and there are those who choose to live like eunuchs for the sake of the kingdom of heaven. The one who can accept this should accept it.
>
> *19:11-12*

Jesus was asking some to do what he himself had perhaps resolved years earlier – to renounce marriage for the sake of the kingdom, the rule of God in his life. He had come to summon Israel to return to God and this completely consumed him. For him, this was what it meant to "seek first the kingdom of God and his righteousness" *(Matthew 6:33)*.

At one level, therefore, Jesus did not marry because he was already in covenant with God. The Father was his companion, and the Spirit his partner and friend; their presence in his life lessened the need for human companionship and enabled him to remain focused on his objectives. In his discussion with the Pharisees, Jesus affirmed the centrality of marriage in God's plan when he quoted from Genesis, so he was clearly not against marriage. At the same time, he set out a manner of life for himself and all others called to singleness. It must have surprised his hearers when Jesus referred to himself as a bridegroom. In conversation with his disciples, Jesus asked them:

> How can the guests of the bridegroom fast while he is with them? They cannot, so long as they have him with them. But the time will come when the bridegroom will be taken from them, and on that day they will fast.
>
> *Mark 2:19-20*

He also spoke of himself in the parable of the wise and foolish virgins as a bridegroom who would return to them: "The bridegroom was a long time in coming ... the bridegroom arrived" *(Matthew 25:5,10)*.

Why did he refer to himself in such terms? Jesus never married because he came to establish a relationship that far transcended a marriage to any one individual. Yet it could nevertheless be best described in terms of a marriage since it would be an exclusive, loving, covenant relationship between two parties. He could not marry one person because, in a sense, he was committed to all who would respond to the invitation to be his bride. We have no way of knowing, of course, when Jesus settled on this conviction; he may have wrestled with it long and hard. Surely he experienced the desires of any normal person and the pressures of those around him, as "one who has been tempted in every way, just as we are" *(Hebrews 4:15)*. Perhaps even the jibes of brothers and sisters might have been awkward, and at times become a source of struggle.

In the following adaptation of *Genesis 2:18-25* (the account of God's creation of woman) I seek to provide an interpretative key to understanding God's purpose and plans in forming the future bride of Christ. Might Jesus have drawn a similar parallel from his own meditations on this scripture?

> Then the Lord God said, "It is not good for my Son to be alone; I will make a companion suitable for him." And out of the heavens, the Father formed every cherub and seraph, and every angel of the sky, and brought them to his Son to see what he would call them; and whatever the Son called one of the angelic host, that was its name.

> And the Son gave names to all the archangels, and the angelic princes, the seraphim and cherubim, but for the Son of Man there was not found a helper and companion suitable for him. And the Lord God caused a deep sleep to fall upon the Man for three days. And he slept in the tomb. Then from the wound that pierced his side, God formed a new creation. The Father fashioned into a Bride what was so dearly torn from the heart of his Son and brought the Bride to his Son. And as he rose triumphant from the sleep of death, the Son of Man jubilantly cried,

> "This is now bone of my bones,
> And flesh of my flesh
> With whom I can be totally one,

108

She shall be called my 'Body of Christ,'
Because she was taken out of the Christ."

For this cause, the Son left the Father and cleaved to his Bride, the church; and they shall become one in spirit. And the Son and his Bride were in perfect harmony and found fulfilment in each other.

Jesus' heart and message echoed that of the Hebrew prophets when they spoke of a God betrothed to his people. Hosea, for example, proclaimed:

"In that day," declares the Lord, "you will call me 'my husband'; you will no longer call me 'my master.' I will remove the names of the Baals from her lips; no longer will their names be invoked ... I will betroth you to me forever; I will betroth you in righteousness and justice, in love and compassion. I will betroth you in faithfulness, and you will acknowledge the Lord."

Hosea 2:16-20

The betrothal of Jesus to his bride is rooted in his compassionate character. Since God is love *(1 John 4:7)*, and all the fullness of God lived in Jesus' bodily form *(Colossians 1:19)*, the life he lived before God and man was the embodiment of love. He perfectly demonstrated the loving character of his Father and the Spirit. Love is not just the explanation for some of Jesus' actions and words, rather it embraces his whole life. Nothing Jesus said or did was contrary to love. The apostle Paul echoes this theme in writing to the believers in Ephesus about the love between a husband and wife *(Ephesians 5:25-32)* and uses this to illustrate the mystery of Christ and the church.

The Bible begins and ends with a marriage. In Genesis it takes place on earth, in Revelation we read of the Bride of Christ in heaven *(Revelation 19:7-8)*; both the marriage of Adam to Eve and Christ to his bride originated in the heart of God. The former symbolises and prefigures the latter; for in the creation of a partner suitable for Adam, we come to see why God created man. The longing of God's heart was expressed. Adam desired one with whom he could enjoy friendship and fellowship. God himself earnestly sought after the company of the redeemed as his Bride.

This is the "profound mystery" Paul brings out in *Ephesians 5:32*. God has no needs, save the 'necessity' to express his character of love. This insight set the course for Jesus' thoughts and actions, ultimately determining his own attitude to marriage, and his decision to remain single. Love was his identity, teaching, and mission. Love was his "most excellent way" *(1 Corinthians 12:31)*.

CHAPTER FIFTEEN

First the Natural, Then the Supernatural

The spiritual does not come first, but the natural, and after that the spiritual.

1 Corinthians 15:46

There is no event so commonplace but that God is present within it, always hidden, always leaving you room to recognize him or not, but all the more fascinatingly because of that, all the more compelling and haunting ... Listen to your life. See it for the fathomless mystery that it is. In the boredom and in the pain of it – no less than in the excitement and gladness: touch, taste, smell your way to the holy hidden heart of it, because in the last analysis all moments are key moments, and life itself is grace.

Fredrick Buechner

Faith tells us of things we have never seen and cannot come to know by our natural senses.

St John of the Cross

In order that everything will be made transparent to him, Jesus is himself fully transparent before God. Jesus is thus able to see people as they truly are.

Hans Urs von Balthasar

Many cultures acknowledge the existence of one supreme and good God. While the taint of sin and corruption appears to have affected much, this cannot, it seems, nullify an intuitive awareness in many of a Creator and an awe-inspiring natural order in the universe (see *Romans 1:18-2:16*). Societies appear tarnished, history catalogues human failures and conflicts, humanity's inability to live in peace and harmony; yet even this is insufficient to disguise the imaginative creative splendour of a world that is, in the words of Gerard Manley Hopkins, "charged with the

111

grandeur of God". While sin casts a shadow over the human spirit and darkens understanding, by contrast, Jesus' sinless spirit was alert, awake, and sensitive to the Father's self-disclosure in creation. Jesus would have learned much from the Father's revelation of himself in creation, which in turn would be reflected in the way he would later teach.

Like the psalmist, Jesus drew closer to the Creator through his creation, where "the heavens declare the glory of God, the skies proclaim the work of his hands" *(Psalm 19:1)*. Similarly, he also learned more of the Law-Giver through the Law – God's moral testimony to humanity revealed in the same psalm: "The law of the LORD is perfect, reviving the soul. The statutes of the LORD are trustworthy, making wise the simple" *(Psalm 19:7)*.

The apostle Paul summarised humanity's knowledge of God in the early part of his letter to the Christians in Rome, and also recorded the history of the human race's disobedience and unbelief. While others may reject God's witness in creation and conscience, this was not so for Jesus. Paraphrasing the words of Paul *(cf. Romans 1:20-21)*:

> From the outset of Jesus' life on earth, the Father's invisible qualities – his eternal power and divine nature – were clearly seen, being understood by Jesus from what has been made. And so, because Jesus already knew the Father, he glorified him as God and gave thanks to him; his thinking became purposeful and his wise heart became enlightened still more.

Jesus would have learned about his Father through the creation – God's unwritten revelation of himself, just as he did through the Law of the Lord, the written revelation given to Moses. He would have developed a deep appreciation for the wonders of the created world – a window into the heart of the Creator, one whose goodness, beauty, and truth are so clearly displayed. By responding positively in faith and obedience to a revelation, further truths and insights are unfolded – this can be as true for us as it must have been for Jesus.

It is not insignificant then that in the Sermon on the Mount *(Matthew 5-7)* Jesus repeatedly used everyday objects drawn from his surroundings to illustrate spiritual truths. He referred to birds, fields, sun, sea, thorns and thistles, pigs, sheep, and goats. "See how the flowers of the field grow" *(Matthew 6:28)*, "Look at the birds of the air" *(Matthew 6:26)*, he exhorted. He drew lessons from nature to teach principles of God's dealings with men. Clearly, the Father had spoken to his Son not only through the written word, but through things in the natural world around him.

Jesus referred to God as Father because he was nurtured and brought up by him as his child. Before he was understood as heavenly Father to individual believers, God was Father to Jesus. This was possible through the partnership and activity of the Spirit who continually witnessed to Jesus' spirit the realities in creation of which the Father spoke. The Father was a companion to Jesus – revealing, anointing, impressing upon his mind, and divinely orchestrating moments to teach the Son.

Jesus learned lessons from nature, and in turn taught his followers; as John records:

> I am the true vine, and my Father is the gardener. He cuts off every branch in me that bears no fruit, while every branch that does bear fruit he prunes so that it will be even more fruitful.
>
> *John 15:1-2*

Jesus compared his relationship with his Father to a vine tended by a gardener. This would then be the pattern he taught for his disciples' relationship with him *(15:1-11)*. He first describes his experience in terms of the Father removing and pruning things from his own life. What might the Father "take away" from Jesus? Or, to put this another way, in this perfect partnership, what might Jesus perceive his heavenly Father showing him that could distract or impede his mission in any way?

As an obedient Son, he would then want to submit, and deny himself such privileges, for example: marriage, wealth, a position of power, worldly status, earthly success. Jesus accepted this discipline, choosing to maintain his focus on his Father's priorities. The Father, in turn, actively prompted, directed, guided, and inspired Jesus throughout his life, to ensure the fulfilment of his destiny; all with Jesus' full cooperation. His was a life of self-denial. To adapt Jesus' words to his disciples, "Whoever wants to be my disciple must deny themselves [as I have] and take up their cross [as I will] and follow me [as I have followed the Father]" *(Matthew 16:24)*.

Following this principle of gleaning spiritual truths for followers of Jesus from his own example, we can adapt the directives given to believers by the writer to the Hebrews. This then provides a window into the life of Jesus under his Father's instruction:

Jesus did not regard lightly the discipline of the Lord, nor lose heart when he experienced hardship from him; for the Lord educated the Son whom he loved; and trained him as the child whom he accepted. Jesus endured trials for the sake of discipline. God treated Jesus as his beloved child; for what child is there whom a parent does not discipline? If Jesus had not had that training, in which all children share, he would not have been his true Son.

Moreover, Jesus had human parents to train him, and he respected them. Was he not even more willing to be subject to the Father of spirits and to live! For Joseph and Mary instructed him for a short time for his good, and in this Jesus reflected the Father's holiness. Discipline always seemed painful rather than pleasant at the time, but later it would yield the peaceful fruit of righteousness for Jesus who had been trained by it.

Adapted from Hebrews 12:5-11

As Christians experience both times of sensing God's presence and his absence, seasons of comfort as well as challenge, of joy and of sorrow, so Jesus would have shared these experiences. Yet, in the words of the apostle Paul, he would have been able to say, "I have learned the secret of being content in any and every situation" *(Philippians 4:12)*.

One of Jesus' best-known parables of the kingdom tells about the different types of soil *(Matthew 13:1-23)*. He knew that while some would accept the good seed of the word of God into their lives, others would have struggles and temptations hampering them from doing so. Before he could deliver it to others, Jesus had first to receive the truth of its message into his *own* life – to ensure there would be nothing in him that might hinder his fruitfulness. His *own* heart must be the good soil, ready to receive the word of God.

Jesus would have walked by fields on many occasions. He would have seen people sowing seed and, as he watched it fall, would perhaps have started to see that just as some of the seed was eaten by the birds, so the enemy would snatch his word from those who refused to listen. While with the seed that did take root, some would spring up where the soil was shallow and poor, there would be those who would listen attentively to him and respond with enthusiasm – but as soon as others made fun or ridiculed them for following him, they would quickly turn away. Similarly, as some seed fell where the ground was covered with thorns and weeds, there would be people whose hearts were like this also. Some would hear and initially want to follow his teaching, but just as weeds spring up and choke the seedlings, so people are caught up in the things of this world, and these concerns prevent his words of life from thriving. However, just as the sower expects to harvest wheat in abundance from the good soil, so Jesus' words would produce the results in his people's lives for the kingdom of God.

And so revelation came to Jesus, gentle, convincing, enlightening, as the scriptures said would happen; revelation he would later share with his closest followers, that they too would come to understand what the ancient writings foretold *(Luke 24:27,45)*. For God had promised a new covenant:

> I will put my law in their minds and write it on their hearts. I will be their God, and they will be my people. No longer will they teach their neighbor, or say to one another, "Know the Lord," because they will all know me, from the least of them to the greatest.
>
> *Jeremiah 31:33-34*

The Father had kept his promise, placing his laws in Jesus' mind, writing them upon his heart.

Jesus, the greatest in the kingdom of heaven, became least among men, humbling himself, and becoming as a little child *(Matthew 18:4)*. He fully exemplified the New Covenant – the new agreement God was making with the human race. At every stage in his growing years, Jesus responded perfectly to the Father without once losing the childlike acceptance he would later commend to his disciples *(Matthew 19:14)*. The Father spoke, the Spirit communicated, and the Son heard and treasured those words in his heart. He never doubted what was revealed. The Spirit confirmed the sonship of Jesus and enriched his relationship with the Father. Like Abraham, it could be said of Jesus that...

> ...he did not waver through unbelief regarding the promise of God, but was strengthened in his faith and gave glory to God, being fully persuaded that God had power to do what he had promised.
>
> *Romans 4:20-21*

Jesus pioneered and perfectly modelled the process for receiving God's truth, so that now every child of God can seek to follow his example. His development from boy to manhood provides us with a flawless pattern and illustrates that, at each stage in our own lives, prayer need not be a series of isolated events. Rather, a believer's prayer life can be an open, continuous channel of communication with the heavenly Father; a moment-by-moment walking in the Spirit, as he bears witness to our own adoption as God's sons and daughters *(Romans 8:16; Galatians 4:6-7)*. What was true in Jesus' experience is now true for us. The Spirit draws us into the fellowship between Father and Son *(1 John 1:3)*. His goal is love and fellowship, unity and peace – with himself and between believers *(1 Corinthians 1:10; Ephesians 4:2)*.

As we explore these truths, a picture increasingly emerges of Jesus less like a saintly mystic in stained glass, or an ethereal spiritual being of super-goodness. More and more we see a man: a real, living, breathing, practical person, guided by a heavenly Father, enlightened and empowered by a faithful, ever-present Counselor and Friend, the Spirit.

We first read of the Holy Spirit described like a protective bird providing for her young, hovering over the waters at creation *(Genesis 1:2)*. In a similar way, the Spirit brooded over the new creation – the incarnation and development of Jesus, from conception through to adulthood, nurturing and bringing into reality a self-awareness and understanding of his own deity and destiny. By the crucial time of Jesus' baptism by John in the river Jordan, everything was in place; this was the moment Jesus had been prepared for. It was as if the starting gun was fired and the Son, with the blessing of the Spirit hovering upon him, was released to fulfil all that had been set before him. The Son received the limitless Spirit; "For the one whom God has sent speaks the words of God, for God gives the Spirit without limit" *(John 3:34)*. This sentiment was echoed by the fourth century theologian Augustine: "The Lord Jesus himself has not only, as God, given the Holy Spirit, but also as a man, he has received him."[130]

With the Spirit's appearance in the form of a dove at his baptism, a new phase began in Jesus' life. Yet at each stage until that moment, the Spirit had already been creatively involved in his life; was instrumental in his birth, guiding him through childhood and early manhood –

---

[130] St Augustine, *The Trinity*, in *The Faith of the Early Fathers*: ed. W. A. Jurgens, 1680

prompting, enlightening, filling, and empowering him. Jesus, the Son of God, had "emptied" himself of his divine attributes, now to live in solidarity with humanity, and to depend on the Spirit's resources.

The central importance of the role of the Holy Spirit is clear from the way Gospel writers repeatedly connect Jesus with the Spirit on many occasions in his life, for example, his conception *(Luke 1:35)*, intimations of his birth *(Luke 1:67, 2:25-27)*, childhood growth *(Luke 1:80)*, prophesied ministry *(Mark 1:8; Matthew 3:11)*, baptism *(Matthew 3:16; Mark 1:10; Luke 3:22)*, temptation *(Matthew 4:1; Mark 1:12; Luke 4:1)*, filling of the Spirit for ministry *(Luke 4:16)*, preaching *(Luke 4:18)*, healing *(Acts 10:38)*, casting out of demons *(Matthew 12:28)*, offering up himself for death *(Hebrews 9:14)*, and resurrection *(Romans 1:4, 8:11; Colossians 2:12)*. The presence of the Spirit was of paramount importance to all that Jesus accomplished.

Since the Holy Spirit was so involved in revealing God's truth to Jesus, how did this affect his own human spirit? From the time of his conception, his human spirit was clear and pure, untainted by sin. Paul's word to the Corinthians could be no truer than when applied to Jesus: "...whoever is united with the Lord is one with him in spirit" *(1 Corinthians 6:17)*.

It is interesting to consider the link between the roles of the mind (cognitive awareness) and the spirit (intuitive perception). While we can accept that Jesus was never confused about who he was, nevertheless his mind had to be enlightened in order to align with his spiritual consciousness. Everything necessary was present from the beginning, but time was essential to allow his mind to fully comprehend what his spirit bore witness to. Divine and human factors must have intertwined in this process – the Spirit's witness validating the testimony of parents and scripture through reflection and revelation. Jesus focused on the invisible, eternal realm. Using Paul's words, he chose to "fix [his] eyes not on what is seen, but on what is unseen, since what is seen is temporary, but what is unseen is eternal" *(2 Corinthians 4:18)*. In Jesus, the Word and the Spirit perfectly came together, bearing witness of divine truth to his own mind and spirit.

Before teachers can teach, they themselves must be taught and trained. This was as true for Jesus as for anyone. Isaiah captures this beautifully in a prophecy that can readily be applied to Jesus as a disciple: "He wakens me morning by morning, wakens my ear to listen like one being instructed" *(Isaiah 50:4)*. It was surely through such Old Testament scriptures that Jesus' self-knowledge would have grown, under the careful tutelage of the Holy Spirit. Then would he be able to say, "He who sent me is trustworthy, and what I have heard from him I tell the world" *(John 8:26)*.

Hans Urs von Balthasar, Swiss intellectual and theologian, supports this view, writing of Jesus' "twofold growth in self-awareness", that he grew in his knowledge of the historical traditions of which he was a part and simultaneously experienced an "interior growth in an awareness of the horizon of his mission"; so that which was "formerly implicit becomes explicit". Jesus' mission was not laid out in its totality before him; he could not anticipate its exact content. Thus the element of prayer was a vital requirement for Jesus. Every important event in his life and mission involved prayer. It was in prayer to the Father that his mission was communicated to him through the Holy Spirit, in stages which fitted into the divine assignment as a whole.

At a crucial time in his ministry, Jesus challenged his disciples at Cæsarea Philippi with a question about his identity that is central to the gospel: "Who do you say that I am?" *(Mark 8:29)*. What more down-to-earth subject needed illumination than this fundamental issue that would set him apart from all others? Before he could challenge others about his identity, he had first to be sure himself: "Who am I?" Jesus' confidence and security in who he was surely developed over the years as he had relied upon the resources of heaven to enlighten him. The Spirit had borne witness to his own spirit, rather like Jewish priests under the old covenant were conscious of the anointing they had received when precious oil was poured upon them *(cf. Psalm 133)*. To adapt John's words:

> Jesus has an anointing from the Holy One, and knows the truth ... The anointing he received lives in him ... and his anointing teaches him about all things.
>
> *cf. 1 John 2:20, 27*

The Spirit enlightened, equipped, and empowered Jesus for his mission. Again, words written later to believers can be adapted and applied in order to glimpse this process:

> That which no eye had seen, no ear had heard, no mind had conceived – which God had prepared for those who love him – all this was revealed to Jesus by the Spirit. The Spirit

searched all things, even the deep things of God and communicated these to Jesus' spirit within him ... He received not the spirit of the world, but the Spirit who is from God, that he might understand what God had freely given him. This enabled Jesus to discern and later to express publicly spiritual truths in spiritual words. As the spiritual man, he made judgments about all things, but was not himself subject to any man's judgment. He had come to know the mind of the Lord as the Spirit instructed him.

Based on 1 Corinthians 2:9-16

When the time came for Jesus to more fully reveal the personality of the Spirit to his disciples on his last evening with them *(John 14:16-17)*, he spoke about the intimacy of their relationship; as he depended totally upon the Father, so too did he depend upon the Spirit. Jesus chose a term that covers a rainbow of meanings: the Spirit was his *Paraclete* – literally, one 'called alongside', in order to counsel, comfort, help, guide, encourage, and intercede for Jesus. In the eternal Trinity we understand that God is not solitary but in a loving communion, a relational circle – dynamic, alive, and characterised by the fullest expression of life. While on earth, Jesus, as the Son, experienced God as Father and the Spirit as Counsellor.

On that last evening with his friends, Jesus told them that they too could share such intimacy and fellowship with God *(John 13-17)*: abundant overflowing life as children of the Father, under the watchful care of the Spirit as Guide and Advocate. Jesus also prepared them for his own ascension, assuring them of his ongoing presence as heavenly Friend and Intercessor *(Romans 8:24; Hebrews 7:25)*. As the Spirit had taught Jesus about all things, he would do the same for his followers.

> The Advocate, the Holy Spirit, whom the Father will send in my name, will teach you all things, and will remind you of everything that I have said to you.
>
> *John 14:26*

> When the Advocate comes, whom I will send to you from the Father – the Spirit of truth who goes out from the Father – he will testify about me.
>
> *John 15:26*

119

> When he, the Spirit of truth, comes, he will guide you into all
> the truth. He will not speak on his own; he will speak only
> what he hears, and he will tell you what is yet to come.
>
> *John 16:13*

Wonderful and amazing as this process was by which Jesus was enlightened and empowered by the Holy Spirit, even more so perhaps is the fact that the Spirit is able to do the same today for his followers. The Body of Christ – his Church, his Bride – experiences the same illumination and equipping so that we too may know "the mind of the Lord". "'For who has known the mind of the Lord so as to instruct him?' But we have the mind of Christ" *(1 Corinthians 2:16)*.

CHAPTER SIXTEEN

Treasures Old and New

In the Old Testament the New lies concealed, in the New Testament the Old is revealed.

Augustine of Hippo

Hear, O Israel: The LORD our God, the LORD is one. Love the LORD your God with all your heart and with all your soul and with all your strength. These commandments that I give you today are to be upon your hearts. Impress them on your children. Talk about them when you sit at home and when you walk along the road, when you lie down and when you get up. Tie them as symbols on your hands and bind them on your foreheads. Write them on the door frames of your houses and on your gates.

Deuteronomy 6:4-9

"Hear, O Israel" begins the *Shema*, the great confession of faith of the Jewish people. It is followed by the injunction for parents to instruct children in God's word. As devout Jews, Joseph and Mary would have 'impressed' them on Jesus and their other children, as this text encourages, talking about scriptural truths in and outside the home throughout the day, as the occasion arose.

There was further opportunity to receive instruction of course on the Sabbath. At the start of Jesus' ministry, we read, "On the Sabbath day, he went into the synagogue, as was his custom" *(Luke 4:16)*. For a period of 27 or so years, Jesus would have regularly attended Sabbath services in the synagogue at Nazareth with his family and been exposed to readings and exposition of the ancient Hebrew scriptures – particularly from the Torah, the first five books of God's word.

Since the time of the Babylonian exile, the Jews had given great attention to the public reading of the Torah. Different schemes were used to break it up into manageable units and at the time of Jesus it was

121

common to divide the Pentateuch into 175 sections, completing its reading aloud in the synagogues over a period of three years. So, between the ages of five and 12, Jesus would have heard the whole cycle through twice, from the Creation to the death of Moses. Read aloud in Hebrew, and also paraphrased and expounded in Aramaic – Jesus' everyday language – the scriptures would have become part of the fabric of his life. Jesus would have committed much of it to memory. It would have been exceedingly unlikely that his own family owned a copy of their own since only the wealthy could afford copies in those days, since parchment was so expensive. Nevertheless, copies of some passages would have formed a cherished treasure of every devout household.

Except for certain sections, which were copied for the instruction of children, it was considered unlawful for anyone other than scribes to make copies of most parts of scripture, so that the integrity of the text was preserved. Permissible sections included the history of Creation to the flood. *Leviticus 1-9* and *Numbers 1-10:35* are also specially mentioned. If this were the case, then we can imagine Joseph reading these ancient records to his children, and his sons copying and reading them to one another. Such training in the scriptures encouraged a reverence for the Law and also honed skills of close, critical study, forming a powerful bond uniting Jewish people.

What impression might the writings of the Torah, the first five books of Hebrew scriptures, have made on Jesus? Let us take, as an example, the familiar account of Abraham being asked to sacrifice his son, Isaac:

> God said, "Take your son, your only son, Isaac, whom you love, and sacrifice him as a burnt offering." When Abraham had cut enough wood for the burnt offering, he set out for the place God had told him about.
>
> On the third day Abraham took the wood and placed it on his son and he himself carried the fire.
>
> As the two of them went on together, Isaac spoke up. "Father?" "Yes, my son?" Abraham replied. "The fire and wood are here," Isaac said, "but where is the lamb for the burnt offering?" Abraham answered, "God himself will provide the lamb for the burnt offering, my son."
>
> When they reached the place God had told him about, Abraham built an altar there and arranged the wood on it. He

bound his son Isaac and laid him on the altar, on top of the wood. Then he reached out his hand and took the knife to slay his son.

But the angel of the Lord called out to him from heaven, "Abraham! Abraham!" "Here I am," he replied. "Do not lay a hand on the boy," he said. "Do not do anything to him. Now I know that you fear God, because you have not withheld from me your son, your only son."

Abraham looked up and there in a thicket he saw a ram caught by its horns. He went over and took the ram and sacrificed it as a burnt offering instead of his son. So Abraham called that place "The Lord Will Provide". And to this day it is said, "On the mountain of the Lord it will be provided."

The angel of the Lord called to Abraham from heaven a second time and said, "I swear by myself, declares the Lord, that because you have done this and have not withheld your son, your only son, I will surely bless you and make your descendants as numerous as the stars in the sky and as the sand on the seashore. Through your offspring all nations on earth will be blessed, because you have obeyed me."

Adapted from Genesis 22:2-18

As he listened, might Jesus have heard the whisper of another in his spirit; heaven speaking – the Father teaching the Son in the power of the Spirit? Did the Spirit affirm to the young Son of Man that the words of this scripture would be fulfilled in his life and death? It is not hard to believe that the seeds of God's word were planted, nurtured, and watered by the Spirit as Jesus came to understand that, indeed, he was the Lamb required for the sacrifice *(Genesis 22:7)*. As this passage was being interpreted to him, did something even stir within Jesus as a distant recollection of the event itself 2,000 years before? For as he later said to those who criticised him for healing a blind man, "Before Abraham was, I AM" *(John 8:58)*.

While what follows is conjecture, it is not implausible if we are to take seriously the role of the Word and the Spirit in Jesus' life. How might Jesus have responded to this text from Genesis? Might some of these questions have gone through his mind?

- I have not read the word "love" before this passage in Genesis. It is a strong word for a father to use for his only son who he believes he has been called to kill. Yet I am God's Son, loved by my Father. Must I give my life as a burnt offering?
- Mount Moriah – the elders say that this is where Jerusalem is now built. Is this where the sacrifice is to occur?
- The son carries the wood that will be used for his execution. Am I to be this Isaac?
- We are not as other nations who sacrifice their children. A spotless lamb is what is required. But am I to be that lamb who dies?
- So this is what it must come to – my death is necessary. I can only submit – even if I cannot comprehend what is to happen.
- Obedience is better than sacrifice. God tests our hearts, and look, he has provided... On the mountain of the Lord it will be provided – so here on a hilltop of Jerusalem, God will accomplish his purposes through me. And if I am to be that one who dies it cannot be the end, for God has promised me descendants.
- God will provide, and the sacrifice and suffering of the Son – and the Father and Spirit – will be the cause of blessing to countless millions in the future.

Long before his relative John had cried out, "Look, the Lamb of God, who takes away the sin of the world!" *(John 1:29)*, Jesus must have learned this was his calling. For years he had faithfully attended the pilgrim festivals, all of which foretold something about his ministry. For example, the great feast of Passover at Jerusalem pointed towards Jesus as the new Moses, who would lead God's people on a spiritual exodus, from slavery to the prince of darkness. He was also the Passover lamb that must be slain for the people, a willing sacrifice as he lay down his life for others *(Mark 10:45)*.

Jesus would have come to realise that he was the Messiah, the one who through his life, death, and resurrection was to bring to fulfilment the Old Testament story. He was to represent and personify Israel, accomplishing her mission as "a light to the nations" *(Isaiah 51:4, 60:3)*. Through him God would make saving grace available to all nations, thereby fulfilling his original promise to Abraham. As predicted, *Yahweh* – God himself – would bring redemption and judgment; the blind would see, the deaf hear, the lame walk, and the dumb speak *(Isaiah 35:4-5; cf. Matthew 11:4-6)*.

Although not until after Peter's confession at Cæsarea Philippi did Jesus give predictions of his death and resurrection (for example, *Mark 8:31, 9:31, 10:33,45*), it seems he knew this was his destiny before then (see *John 2:21*). Knowledge of scripture in passages like *Isaiah 53* and *Psalm 22* in his teenage years would have laid a clear foundation for his understanding, and his confrontation with Satan in the wilderness may have brought this into sharp relief. From awareness of his unique identity and his calling to teach and model God's kingdom life, Jesus came, too, to the realisation of what he must suffer in order to rescue humanity from alienation into a full experience of the life of God.

We have noted that, living in Galilee, Jesus would in all probability have read scripture in Hebrew, conversed in Aramaic, while having a smattering of Greek (as well as possibly some Latin, the official language of the occupying Roman forces). Although we have no evidence that he trained in a rabbinical school – a Jewish school of higher education *(John 7:15)* – his knowledge and understanding of the scriptures was extensive. Since the Pharisees and Sadducees always referred to the original Hebrew texts, Jesus could have done no less. Such was his confidence in scripture that he could challenge the experts with remarks such as, "Have you not read?" *(Matthew 12:3,5; Mark 12:10, 12:26; Luke 6:3)*; an assurance first evidenced, as we have seen, as a twelve-year-old *(Luke 2:49)*.

Near the outset of his ministry Jesus claimed that he had come to fulfil the Law and the Prophets *(Matthew 5:17)*. At the close of his earthly vocation he could truly claim to have accomplished what he had set out to do: "It is finished" *(John 19:30)*. Not that he set out from the dawn of consciousness to fulfil Old Testament prophecy in some rigid, mechanistic way; rather that – while fully aware of those prophecies – Jesus was so conscious of God's hand in his life that in a free and natural way, he determined to live out all the Father had planned for him.

As the prophets "who spoke of the grace that was to come ... searched intently and with the greatest care" *(1 Peter 1:10)* concerning salvation, so too did Jesus dig deeply into the scriptures. Like those before him, he sought "to find out the time and circumstances to which the Spirit of Christ in them was pointing when he predicted the sufferings of Christ and the glories that would follow" *(1 Peter 1:11)*. If "it was revealed to [the prophets] ... by the Holy Spirit" how much more did the Spirit reveal to Jesus these same truths "into which angels long to look"? *(1 Peter*

1:12). It could be said that, as the pre-existent Word and divine Inspirer of scripture, Jesus read the outline of his biography before the events it describes took place.

Philip Yancey reminds us that the Old Testament contains the prayers Jesus prayed, the poems he memorised, the songs he sang, the bedtime stories he heard as a child and the prophecies he pondered. Jesus revered every 'jot and tittle' – "the smallest letter ... least stroke of the pen" of the Hebrew scriptures *(Matthew 5:18)*, so much so that in fact the more we comprehend the Old Testament, the more we comprehend him.

The entire sweep of the Old Testament is preparatory for, and predictive of, Jesus and his kingdom. The predictions are not isolated but are features on a much broader prophetic canvas; the institutions and rituals part of one grand system. The revelatory history is not a series of loosely connected events, but a development moving towards a defined goal – the establishing of God's rule upon the earth through the Messiah. Each part is messianic by way of preparing for the coming of Christ. It functions as a *paidagogos* – conductor of children (or "school master" as it reads in the older translation) – to lead the nation to Christ *(Galatians 3:24, 4:25)*.

Martin Luther, the German theologian who was a major catalyst for the Reformation, referred to the Old Testament as "a testamental letter of Christ, which he caused to be opened after his death and read and proclaimed everywhere through the Gospel."[131] Old Testament history served as a preparation for Jesus, with the characters on its pages contributing a family, an identity, and a race for Jesus to be born into. Thus we now come to appreciate that the most important person ever to read the Old Testament was surely Jesus himself. Scripture was divinely inspired and ordained, enabling Jesus to come to full self-understanding, and to provide him with an inexhaustible treasure during those 10,000 days before his ministry.

> All scripture is God-breathed and is useful for teaching, rebuking, correcting and training in righteousness, so that the servant of God may be thoroughly equipped for every good work.
>
> *2 Timothy 3:16-17*

---

[131] Quoted by Yancey, *The Bible Jesus Read,* 25

Since Jesus' role was vital to God's plan of salvation, we might even say that scripture was written primarily – though not of course exclusively – for him. It was the Father's supreme teaching resource, providing Jesus with a blueprint and plan for God's redemptive program, and thus for his life's work. In the passages of the Old Testament, Jesus could trace every important fact about himself and his mission. He quoted from it in order to settle controversies, to silence opponents – even Satan himself – and used its images to define himself: Lamb of God, Good Shepherd, the sign of Jonah, the Bread from heaven, the Water of life.

The scriptures would have challenged, comforted, and encouraged the living Word, Jesus, preparing him for his life's work. His unique communion with the Father guided him at every point and this intuitive direction was supported and filled out by the divine blueprint for Messiah's ministry found in the scriptures. That which he learned about himself and others was corroborated by the Father and the Spirit, bringing into sharper focus his ministry, mission, and destiny *(Matthew 5:17; Luke 24:27,44; John 5:39)*.

Jesus pioneered and perfected the art of interpreting scripture, paving the way for the New Testament writers. His approach to scripture would be the creative inspiration and model for those who would later write down the good news – Matthew, Mark, Luke, and John, and the instructional, pastoral letters of Paul and other writers to believers. Jesus' grasp of scripture remains unparalleled. As the great interpreter of God's revelation, he distilled its wisdom, refashioned its words and images, and then spoke out the message of God in powerful words unsurpassed since. In him "are hidden all the treasures of wisdom and knowledge" *(Colossians 2:3)*.

Jesus was also skilful in the technicalities of legal debate. His interpretations were so radically different from that of other rabbis; they were astounded that someone who had never attended their formal rabbinic schools could nevertheless teach and debate in a way superior to their most highly trained professionals.

Jesus' teachings would indeed prove to be the new wine that would burst the old wineskins; the new cloth which would tear away from an old garment *(Mark 2:21-22)*. Based on his own experience he would later teach others:

> Every teacher of the law who has become a disciple in the
> kingdom of heaven is like the owner of a house who brings
> out of his storeroom new treasures as well as old.
>
> *Matthew 13:52*

For 10,000 days Jesus, the obedient disciple, had been gathering nuggets of gold from the riches of the Law and the Prophets. Now as "owner of the house", he was dispensing them.

For Jesus, the Old Testament was true, authoritative and inspired, the immutable word of God – so precious to him that we see quotations or references to 39 Old Testament passages, from 16 books, in Luke's Gospel alone. The quotations in all four Gospels are predominantly from Deuteronomy, Psalms, and Isaiah. Altogether Jesus quoted from at least 24 different Old Testament books. The God of the Old Testament was his heavenly Father, and the truths it contained were his Father's teaching *(Matthew 22:29; John 10:35)*. For him, what scripture said, the living God said.

It was indeed "treasure from the storeroom" of the Psalms and the prophet Isaiah that would most nurture his mind and spirit, giving purpose and direction to his own mission as he prepared to enter the public arena of ministry. With unprecedented authority Jesus demonstrated himself to be the pivot of history, to which all previous events had led, now heralding in an increase of the kingdom of God into the world.

"You study the Scriptures diligently because you think that in them you have eternal life. These are the very Scriptures that testify about me, yet you refuse to come to me to have life" *(John 5:39-40)*. "All the prophets testify about him," declared Peter *(Acts 10:43)*. As the Old Testament had pointed toward him, Jesus now showed how the scriptures find their ultimate validity in him and his teaching.

CHAPTER SEVENTEEN

Jesus Reads the Psalms

David was a prophet ... Seeing what was to come, he spoke of ... the Christ.

Acts 2:30-31

What various and resplendent riches are contained in this treasury! [It is ...] an anatomy of all parts of the soul; for there is not an emotion of which any one can be conscious that there is not here represented as in a mirror.

John Calvin

To return to the task we set out initially: Jesus had 10,000 days to reflect on three fundamental questions concerning the messiah, his message, and his mission: Who am I? What should I do? Why have I come to earth? In what ways did he use those 10,000 days to discover answers about his identity, his calling, and that which lay ahead for him to accomplish? This chapter explores the insights Jesus would have gleaned from one significant part of the Old Testament – the Book of Psalms.

Almost one third of the quotations from the Hebrew Bible in the New Testament (112 of 360) are taken from the Psalms. "The Psalter is the most important book of the Old Testament in terms of its testimony to Christ," writes theologian Geoffrey W. Grogan. Of the 19 citations by Jesus from the Old Testament he quotes most frequently from the book of Psalms. These psalms he had grown up with provided an interpretative framework for so much of what he would come to realise and experience. Six psalms relate to the last week of his life: his triumphal entry *(Psalm 8:2; Matthew 21:16)*; his parable about Israel *(Psalm 118:22-23; Matthew 21:42,44)*; his response to questioning about his identity in the Temple *(Psalm 110:1; Mark 12:36)*; the Passover *(Psalms 35:19, 69:4; John 15:25)*; and his words on the cross *(Psalm 22:1; Matthew 27:46, 31:5; Luke 23:46)*. Events that took place just days before his resurrection are interpreted by Jesus in passages he had come to treasure.

129

By tracing Jesus' pilgrimage from his childhood, we can imagine how he began to enjoy this richest of Old Testament treasures, the book of Psalms, and how this shaped both his life and his outlook on the world. As he sought to be obedient to what he read, the words must have taken on a very personal and, at times, autobiographical character. Through the psalms he learned more about his Father, his place in redemption, and humanity. His messianic self-awareness was fostered by many psalms; he would fulfil them and they in turn would be fulfilled in him.

None of the psalms were actually written *by* Jesus, though some use words he would one day quote (for example, *Psalm 22:1*). Some appear almost to be written *to* Jesus – to prepare him for what lay ahead and to increase his self-understanding; some were written *about* him – to prepare others to understand him better. But, in one sense, all were written (ultimately) *for* Jesus – to inform him, increasing his self-understanding, and bringing awareness of his identity and his mission.

By exploring the book of Psalms through the eyes of Jesus, we see how they shaped his life and teachings: those that resonated with his life-situation, those he most quoted, and those which opened up a perspective prophetically that he would need later in his ministry. As Scott McKnight writes:

> Jesus was a master of the Psalms. Whenever he heard them, in the synagogue and at the Temple, he took them to heart, for the Psalms spilled constantly from his lips ... His entire life was bathed with Psalms ... Jesus prayed the Psalms and Christians have always followed his example.[132]

Similarly, Bonhoeffer encouraged Christian students to pray the psalms of Christ as the prayers of Christ:

> The *Man* Jesus Christ, to whom no affliction, no ill, no suffering is alien and who yet was the wholly innocent and righteous one, is praying in the Psalter through the mouth of his church. The Psalter is the prayer book of Jesus Christ in the truest sense of the word. He prayed the Psalter and now it has become his prayer for all time ... The Psalter is the vicarious prayer of Christ for his church.

---

[132] Scott McKnight, *Praying with the Church,* p.53

After his resurrection, Luke records:

> And beginning with Moses and all the Prophets, he explained
> to them what was said in all the Scriptures concerning himself.
>
> *Luke 24:27*

> He said to them, "This is what I told you while I was still with
> you: everything must be fulfilled that is written about me in
> the Law of Moses, the Prophets and the Psalms." Then he
> opened their minds so they could understand the Scriptures.
>
> *Luke 24:44-45*

Jesus "conversed", "discussed", "debated", "opened up", and
"explained" the scriptures. He taught his disciples systematically and
comprehensively ("beginning with Moses and all the prophets"),
explaining the meaning of passages that pointed towards him, plus others
that had provided the basis for his self-understanding. From the writings
of Moses the lawgiver, Isaiah the prophet, and David the psalmist, for
example, each alluding to the coming Messiah, the redeemer of God's
people and Saviour for the whole world (for example, see *John 5:46,
12:41; Mark 12:35-37*), Jesus shared insights he had gleaned from
studying the scriptures since childhood. As a young boy, he had amazed
trained rabbis with his mastery of the Law *(Luke 2:46-47)*; twenty years
later, his knowledge was complete, and we read that "he opened the
minds" of the disciples, so they could share this understanding.

About 15 psalms are cited in the New Testament in connection with
the Messiah, yet approximately 36 are referred to as "messianic psalms"
since they point ahead to the coming Saviour. David himself – shepherd,
poet, king – to some extent foreshadowed the Messiah; despite his frailty
as a sinful human, David was a "man after God's own heart" *(1 Samuel
13:14)*. How fascinating it would be to know which psalms Jesus used
when he opened the scriptures to the weary travellers on the road to
Emmaus *(Luke 24:32)*.

As Martin Luther observed:

> The Psalter ... promises Christ's death and resurrection so
> clearly – and pictures his kingdom and the condition and
> nature of all Christendom – that it might well be called a little

131

Bible. In it is comprehended most beautifully and briefly everything that is in the entire Bible.[133]

In the Book of Psalms we see Jesus described as God the Son *(2)*, the one chosen by God *(45)*, a teacher of parables *(78)* and a priest forever *(110)*. He is depicted as one who would be betrayed by a friend *(41)*, lied about *(35)*, mocked, tortured, and eventually brutally killed *(22)*. Yet this long-awaited Saviour would come back to life *(16)* then return to heaven to reign with the Father *(68)*. He will come back later to rule over a new heaven and earth forever *(72)*.

Although the Psalter was not strictly considered to be among the prophetic books of the Old Testament, it nevertheless clearly contains several forward-pointing signs of the coming Christ. In some examples the subject is a 'type'[134] of Christ *(34:20, 69:4,9)*. In others, the psalmist used language which pointed beyond his own life and became historically true only in Christ *(22)*. There are others where a king or the throne of David in general was referred to, but the final fulfilment was clearly in Christ *(2, 45, 72)*, and some that can be seen to refer solely to Christ without reference to any other son of David (Psalm 110). A final category anticipated the coming of the Lord and the consummation of his kingdom *(96-99)*.

In this collection of poems and songs we read of Jesus as the *Royal Messiah (2, 18, 20, 21, 45, 61, 72, 89, 110, 132, 144)*, the *Suffering Messiah (22, 35, 41, 55, 69, 109)* and the *Messiah as the Son of Man (16, 40)*. The significance of these writings was not lost on New Testament writers as the following list illustrates.

---

[133] Martin Luther, *Preface to the Psalter* in *Luther's Works*, 35.254

[134] Got Questions.org *(https://www.gotquestions.org/typology-biblical.html)* defines Typology as a special kind of symbolism where one subject is represented by something else. We can define a type as a 'prophetic symbol' since it represents something yet in the future. More specifically, a type in scripture is used for a person (or thing) in the Old Testament that foreshadows someone (or something) in the New Testament. To say that someone in the Old Testament is a type of Christ, is to attribute to them certain characteristics or behaviour in a way that corresponds to that of Jesus.

Psalm	Prophecy	Fulfilment
2:7	God will declare him to be his beloved Son	Matthew 3:17
8:2	Children will praise God's Son	Matthew 21:16
8:4,5	Jesus made lower than the angels	Hebrews 2:6-9
8:6	All things will be put under his feet	Hebrews 2:8
16:10	He will be resurrected from the dead	Mark 16:6,7
22:1	God will forsake him in his hour of need	Matthew 27:46
22:7,8	He will be scorned and mocked	Luke 23:35
22:15	He will thirst while on the cross	John 19:28
22:16	His hands and feet will be pierced	John 20:25,27
22:18	Others will gamble for his garments	Matthew 27:35
22:22	Jesus will declare his name in the church	Hebrews 2:12
31:5	Messiah will commit his spirit to God	Luke 23:46
34:20	Not a bone of his shall be broken	John 19:32,33,36
35:11	He will be accused of false testimony	Mark 14:57
35:19	He will be hated for no good reason	John 15:25
40:7,8	He will come to do God's will	Hebrews 10:7
41:9	He will be betrayed by a friend	Luke 22:47
45:6	His throne will be forever	Hebrews 1:8
68:18	He will ascend to the right hand of God	Mark 16:19
69:9	Zeal for God's house will consume him	John 2:17
69:21	He will be given wine and gall to drink	Matthew 27:34

Psalm	Prophecy	Fulfilment
69:25	Judgment on the Messiah's persecutor	Acts 1:20
78:2	Messiah will speak in parables	Matthew 13:34,35
89:3,4,35,36	He will be a descendant of David	Luke 1:31-33
96:13	He will return to judge the world	1 Thessalonians 1:10
102:25-27	Characteristics of the coming King	Hebrews 1:10-12
109:4	He will pray for his enemies	Luke 23:34
109:8	His betrayer's place will be filled by another	Acts 1:20
110:1	His enemies will be made subject to him	Matthew 22:44
110:1	He is Son, and Lord of David	Matthew 22:41-45
110:4	He will be a priest like Melchizedek	Hebrews 5:6
118:22	He will be the chief cornerstone rejected by many	Matthew 21:42
118:26	He will come in the name of the Lord	Matthew 21:9

As a child, Jesus would have heard the psalms read or sung at home or in the synagogue. As he grew older, there would have been much to meditate upon as he studied them for himself. How closely was he able to identify with the aspirations and desires of the psalmist? How formative were the psalms in fashioning Jesus' self-understanding and role? With the benefit of hindsight, we can trace the chronological sequence as the psalms relate to the life of Jesus, but how much did the Holy Spirit reveal to him before his ministry began?

Psalms 16-24, for example, reflect the character of the godly but find their ultimate fulfilment in Christ. They provide us with prophetic cameos of him and it is not hard to imagine Jesus using these words in prayer. *The Hodder Bible Handbook* gives headings to these nine psalms:

Psalm 16 Christ obedient is resurrected
Psalm 17 Christ the Intercessor
Psalm 18 God's power preserved Christ

Psalm 19 Christ in creation and revelation
Psalm 20 Christ and his salvation
Psalm 21 Christ's kingly glory is anticipated
Psalm 22 Christ's sufferings and coming glory
Psalm 23 Christ the Great Shepherd
Psalm 24 Christ the Chief Shepherd

What a feast Jesus would have found as he meditated upon David's words. Certain psalms mirror events and emotions in Jesus' life, supplementing the New Testament records. *Psalm 22*, for example, reveals more about his thoughts and feelings at his crucifixion than the descriptions given in the Gospels. The cry of Jesus from the cross *(Mark 15:34)* shows us that he had made this psalmist's lament his own. He had descended into the depths of human suffering and was intimately acquainted with the questions asked by sufferers in every age: "Why?" and "How long?"

The writer to the Hebrews quotes *Psalm 40:6-7* and challenges us to look beyond the original intent of David's original words. Here we have a fascinating glimpse of Jesus' revelation when he "came into the world".

Therefore, when Christ came into the world, he said:

"Sacrifice and offering you did not desire,
but a body you prepared for me;
with burnt offerings and sin offerings
you were not pleased.
Then I said, 'Here I am – it is written about me in the scroll –
I have come to do your will, my God.'"

First he said, "Sacrifices and offerings, burnt offerings and sin offerings you did not desire, nor were you pleased with them" – though they were offered in accordance with the law. Then he said, "Here I am, I have come to do your will." He sets aside the first to establish the second. And by that will, we have been made holy through the sacrifice of the body of Jesus Christ once for all.

Hebrews 10:5-10

Perhaps it was on his first Passover pilgrimage to the Temple in Jerusalem, witnessing the slaughter of countless lambs, when the twelve-year-old first realised that "to obey is better than sacrifice" *(1 Samuel*

15:22). Was it then that he offered himself to the Father: "I have come to do your will"? Was it then, from his reading of the Law, that he became aware of his identity and mission: "It is written about me in the scroll"?

The accounts of three groups of people dominate the history of God's people in Old Testament times: prophets, priests, and kings. Moses, Samuel, and David were each chosen and anointed by God to lead and mediate God's relationship with man. Some individuals came close to the leadership and character God desired, but countless others were poor examples – weak priests, corrupt kings, and compromising prophets *(cf. Jeremiah 8:1)*. As the centuries passed, Israel came to believe that God would one day send the Anointed One – the Messiah. He is described in priestly terms *(Psalm 110)*, sometimes as a king *(Psalm 2)*, and also as a prophet *(Deuteronomy 18:15,17)*. The New Testament writers were unanimous in affirming Jesus to be the Messiah Israel longed for, an understanding that can be traced back to Jesus himself, who would have received confirmation of this as he studied the ancient texts. The Psalms, a treasury of David, became a treasury for Jesus.

> You are the most excellent of men
> and your lips have been anointed with grace,
> since God has blessed you forever.
> Your throne, O God, will last for ever and ever;
> a scepter of justice will be the scepter of your kingdom.
> You love righteousness and hate wickedness;
> therefore God, your God, has set you above your companions
> by anointing you with the oil of joy.
>
> *Psalm 45:2,6-7*

Jesus, "the most excellent of men", is none other than God whose throne lasts forever. He has been distinguished from all others by the anointing of the Spirit – with grace and joy, as the New Testament writer to the Hebrews declares:

> "Your throne, O God, will last for ever and ever;
> a scepter of justice will be the scepter of your kingdom.
> You have loved righteousness and hated wickedness;
> therefore God, your God, has set you above your companions
> by anointing you with the oil of joy."
>
> *Hebrews 1:8-9*

To the Jews who sought to kill him for blasphemy, Jesus warned: "You study the Scriptures diligently because you think that in them you have eternal life. These are the very Scriptures that testify about me" *(John 5:39)*. By studying the Psalms we ourselves are challenged by the truth of Jesus' words; as *The Message* translation puts it, "These Scriptures are all about *me*!" To illustrate this, let us look at the psalm that serves as an introduction to all others, a beautiful reflection by someone who has been meditating on God's Law.

> Blessed is the one
> who does not walk in step with the wicked
> or stand in the way that sinners take or sit in the company of mockers,
> but whose delight is in the law of the Lord,
> and who meditates on his law day and night.
> That person is like a tree planted by streams of water,
> which yields its fruit in season
> and whose leaf does not wither – whatever they do prospers.
> Not so the wicked!
> They are like chaff that the wind blows away.
> Therefore the wicked will not stand in the judgment,
> nor sinners in the assembly of the righteous.
> For the Lord watches over the way of the righteous,
> but the way of the wicked leads to destruction.

Psalm 1:1-6

Like the Sermon on the Mount, the book of Psalms begins with a 'beatitude' – a pronouncement of God's blessing on the righteous. *Psalm 1* seems to have made a lasting impression on Jesus. The description of two paths – one followed by the righteous, the other by the wicked – became central to his teaching in the Sermon on the Mount *(Matthew 5-7)*. But long before he taught his disciples how to live, Jesus had personally accepted the teaching not to walk, stand, or sit in the company of those who might lead him astray *(1:1)*.

Martin Luther, the Reformer declared, "The first psalm speaks literally concerning Christ."[135] The focus is on the individual who has made God's word central in his life and so is particularly fitting when we

---

[135] Martin Luther, *First Lectures on the Psalms, Psalms 1-75, Luther's Works,* 10:11

consider Jesus, who lived by "every word that comes from the mouth of God" *(Matthew 4:4)*, and whom John described at the outset of his Gospel as embodying the "Word of God" *(John 1:1)*. Could there be a better description of Jesus' attitude to God's word than that expressed in the opening sentence of this psalm? His delight was in the Law of the Lord; for him, God's word was a source of endless pleasure.

Israel's king was required to keep a copy of the Law and read it daily *(Deuteronomy 17:19)*. Jesus, too, delighted in the Torah and would have studied it avidly at every opportunity. Encouraged from childhood, by his parents and hearing the texts read aloud in the synagogue in Nazareth, Jesus became steeped in the language and history of his people and their God. A child's excitement and joy at first learning to spell out words and then to read would have been multiplied for Jesus as this empowered him to discover the Torah for himself – and to meditate on God's word "day and night".

Jesus was like "a good tree bearing good fruit" and used this image in his Sermon on the Mount *(Matthew 7:16)*. But trees do not bear fruit right away; they must be nourished, and for some it may take many years. Through prayer and meditation Jesus grew in holiness; this required perseverance and patience, so he would "yield good fruit in season". As an adolescent he must have resolved to guard himself carefully from the influence of those who might seek to distract or draw him away from his Father. Thus, even in youth, Jesus was 'known by his fruits', as he grew in wisdom and stature, and in favour with God and man *(Luke 2:52; cf. Psalm 92:13-15; Matthew 7:20)*.

Timing was crucial in those preparation years. Everything Jesus did was 'at the right time' under the direction of the Father and the Spirit *(cf. John 7:8, 16:32; Romans 5:6)*. Throughout Jesus' life on earth, the Lord indeed was "watching over the way" of his Righteous One.

CHAPTER EIGHTEEN

King, Servant, and Disciple

I think Isaiah wrote not a prophecy but a gospel.

Augustine

Isaiah should be called an evangelist rather than a prophet because he describes all the mysteries of Christ and the church so clearly that you would think he is composing a history of what has already happened rather than prophesying about what is to come.

Jerome

Isaiah … saw Jesus' glory and spoke about him.

John 12:41

Isaiah speaks so often of the Messiah, that the book is often called the "Fifth Gospel."[136]

John Sawyer

Just weeks after his baptism Jesus returned to the family home in Nazareth. He had lived here most of his life and would have been known by everyone. As was his custom he went to the synagogue he had attended since childhood. Here he had been taught to read and love the sacred texts; here, like other men from the village, he would have stood to read aloud from the scriptures. Luke records that on this occasion he was handed the scroll of Isaiah and began confidently to read a passage:

---

[136] John F. A. Sawyer, *The Fifth Gospel, Isaiah in the History of Christianity.* The idea of Isaiah as a fifth gospel goes back to Jerome (342-420), Augustine (354-430), Isidore of Seville (560-636), and the influential 13th century exegete, Hugh of St. Cher. By such, Isaiah was viewed as more an evangelist than a prophet, as it seems he anticipated and spelled out most Christian essentials in what would become the 66 chapters of his writing.

[Jesus] went to Nazareth, where he had been brought up, and on the Sabbath day he went into the synagogue, as was his custom. He stood up to read, and the scroll of the prophet Isaiah was handed to him. Unrolling it, he found the place where it is written:

"The Spirit of the Lord is on me, because he has anointed me to proclaim good news to the poor. He has sent me to proclaim freedom for the prisoners and recovery of sight for the blind, to set the oppressed free, to proclaim the year of the Lord's favour."

Then he rolled up the scroll, gave it back to the attendant and sat down. The eyes of everyone in the synagogue were fastened on him. He began by saying to them, "Today this scripture is fulfilled in your hearing."

Luke 4:16-21

The Father had anointed Jesus with the Spirit; he was the Messiah; this was his mission. The shock and tension on the part of those who had known him since infancy must have been palpable. The long-held secret was disclosed and his neighbours and relatives could not take it in.

There were many other messianic prophecies in Isaiah's book that Jesus could have read when he stood up in the synagogue, but the one in the appointed reading for the day was from the last section of Isaiah *(Isaiah 61:1-3)*, sometimes referred to as his manifesto. Isaiah's prophecies were written over 700 years. British theologian, Alex Motyer, groups these around three portraits:

- King *(Isaiah 1-37)*, chapters *7:10-15, 9:1-7, 11:1-16, 14:28-32, 24:21-23, 32:1-8, 33:17-24;*
- Servant of the Lord *(Isaiah 38-55)*, chapters *42:1-4, 49:1-6, 50:4-9, 52:13-53:12;*
- Anointed Conqueror *(Isaiah 56-66)*, chapters *59:21, 61:1-3, 61:10-62:7, 63:1-6.*

"It would be difficult to overstate the importance of Isaiah for the Christology of the church," observed Tremper Longman and Raymond Dillard. Similarly, John Sawyer notes that the book of Isaiah is more often quoted or alluded to in the Gospels, Acts, Paul, and Revelation than any other part of scripture, with the possible exception of the Psalms.

One estimate gives the total number of passages in which Isaiah referred to Jesus as 250.

We can imagine that the Holy Spirit had already highlighted portions of the text and interpreted them to Jesus over previous years – just as with others passages from the *Tanakh*, the Old Testament. We may safely assume that Jesus already knew Isaiah's prophecies well, having listened to them or read them himself many times over the years. Some passages reflected different stages of his earthly pilgrimage, others would have provided a model for him as he faced unique circumstances, and yet others foretold what lay ahead – the awful suffering he must endure and then the glorious future beyond.

> Who has believed our message and to whom has the arm of the LORD been revealed? He grew up before him like a tender shoot, and like a root out of dry ground. He had no beauty or majesty to attract us to him, nothing in his appearance that we should desire him.
>
> *Isaiah 53:1-2*

The analogy is one of natural growth, as a seed from dry ground – somewhat unexpectedly from such unlikely soil. Perhaps this relates to Jesus' ordinary family tree, or the state of the nation at that time – not apparently filled with spiritual fervour or anticipation; there had been so many 'messiahs' who had not delivered! Yet how could a mere man be "the arm of the LORD"? This Servant of the Lord was not noticeably well-built, impressive, or handsome. But, as Samuel was reminded, God does not judge by the way we often do: "People look at the outward appearance, but the LORD looks at the heart" *(1 Samuel 16:7)*. With nothing ostensibly to distinguish Jesus from others, it must have been hard for those from his village to believe that he really was Yeshua – 'the Lord come to save' – a salutary lesson for any culture obsessed with external appearance.

Other predictions in this "Fifth Gospel" help us to understand Jesus better. Consider how Isaiah's words go beyond any description of himself as a person, or Israel as a nation, but resonate with the man Christ Jesus:

> Before I was born the LORD called me; from my mother's womb he has spoken my name. He made my mouth like a sharpened sword, in the shadow of his hand he hid me; he made me into a polished arrow and concealed me in his quiver.

He said to me, "You are my servant, Israel, in whom I will display my splendor." But I said, "I have labored in vain. I have spent my strength for nothing at all. Yet what is due me is in the LORD's hand, and my reward is with my God."

Isaiah 49:1-4

Before birth the Lord had called Jesus, keeping his name secret until it was the right moment to announce, "This is Israel." For Jesus is the true embodiment of Israel, the people of God, throughout the ages. The Son had been prepared by the Father for the words he would deliver "like a sharpened sword or a polished arrow"; the sword for close combat and the arrow for targets further away. Like a polished arrow, Jesus would be free from rough edges that might deflect its accuracy in flight, preparing him in the secret place. For 10,000 days he was "concealed" – hidden from others, in the intimacy of his relationship with his Father, as the obedient Servant of the LORD.

The last verse is the hardest to equate with Jesus' experience: "I have laboured in vain. I have spent my strength for nothing at all." *(49:4a)*. When was Jesus so despondent? Alec Motyer does not consider that the darkness of Gethsemane fits the case, for there his distress arose from the impending events to come, not because of past regrets. But there had been times when Jesus faced malevolent rejection, unbelief, prejudice and misunderstanding – some even before his ministry began. The sadness he must have felt at his own family's vacillating attitude towards him allow us to apply this prophecy to the whole of his life, and not just to the period of his public ministry. Mostly, though, these vehement attacks were from those who distrusted and maligned his ministry, threatened by the recognition he received from the ordinary people.

There was sorrow, too, when even some of Jesus' followers hindered the work by their lack of faith. "You unbelieving and perverse generation, how long shall I stay with you and put up with you?" he cried out *(Luke 9:41)*; times when he could only sigh over the people's continuing failure to understand *(Mark 8:21)*, and when he foresaw the falling away of the inner group *(Mark 14:27)*. "Maybe what was thus diffused throughout our Lord's whole earthly life, Isaiah compresses into a single moment."[137]

---

[137] Alex Motyer, *The Prophecy of Isaiah*, on Isaiah 49:5

Jesus undoubtedly enjoyed some rich friendships in his adult life, though he clearly also had times of isolation and loneliness. No one knew what he knew; no one could do what he had come to do; there was no other human being with whom he could share this. At times his was a solitary path, yet his private life is a model of discipleship. He was disciplined and trained by his Father and his life produced "a harvest of righteousness and peace" *(cf. Hebrews 12:7-11)*.

> The Sovereign LORD has given me a well-instructed tongue, to know the word that sustains the weary. He wakens me morning by morning, wakens my ear to listen like one being instructed. The Sovereign Lord has opened my ears; and I have not been rebellious, I have not turned away.
>
> *Isaiah 50:4-5*

Like the infant Samuel, Jesus learned to discern the Lord speaking to him *(1 Samuel 3:10)*. He had "an instructed tongue", that is, the tongue of one who is taught – a 'disciple's tongue'. Jesus, the Servant, is presented before us as the perfect disciple. This ability to say the right thing was not an instant gift; it came through the training associated with all true discipleship, from concentrating on the word of the Lord. God's faithful instruction had been a daily discipline, "morning by morning", for the greater part of three decades. The sharpened sword and the polished arrow *(Isaiah 49:2)* were not automatic, spontaneous or all at once. This was the outcome of a life of regular and daily appointments in his Father's presence.

Jesus' positive and unashamed response to his Father's instructions demonstrated his true discipleship. His mouth was filled with the appropriate words to say because his ears had been filled with the word of God. Alec Motyer comments:

> There came a moment in the sequence of morning instruction when a particular intimation of the Lord's will was granted and, equally a product of the morning discipleship, it was met by obedience ... We are not told at this point what it was the Lord God called his Servant to do, only that the call was met by a total response of will.

Yet such appointments were not to be considered for the perfect Servant alone; rather, this was intended to be a model, a perfect example, for all who would serve and obey the Lord.

At the Father's instigation, the Spirit came in fullness upon the Son at conception: "For the one whom God has sent speaks the words of God, for God gives the Spirit without limit. The Father loves the Son and has placed everything in his hands" *(John 3:34-35)*. From the outset of his earthly pilgrimage, Jesus enjoyed an unparalleled experience of the Spirit's personality; everything about the Spirit had been placed in his hands. Isaiah confirmed this when he wrote about the sevenfold Spirit resting upon Jesus *(cf. Revelation 1:4)*:

> A shoot will come up from the stump of Jesse; from his roots a Branch will bear fruit. The Spirit of the LORD will rest on him – the Spirit of wisdom and of understanding, the Spirit of counsel and of might, the Spirit of knowledge and fear of the LORD – and he will delight in the fear of the LORD. He will not judge by what he sees with his eyes, or decide by what he hears with his ears;
>
> *Isaiah 11:1-3*

The Spirit who anointed David now touched the One born to rule the house of David *(cf. Jeremiah 23:5f, 30:9, 33:14-16)*. Before the Shoot became a Branch, the Spirit began his work. From seemingly hopeless origins – the lifeless Davidic stump – One greater than David emerged. The "Spirit of the Lord" rested on Jesus. The divine Gardener watched over the maturation process from insignificant beginning to a fruit-bearing Branch. First and foremost, this is the Spirit of Yahweh; the Spirit defining the identity and personality of God the Father to Jesus. He transmitted, transfused, and transferred his essence and heart to the Son.

The "Spirit of wisdom and of understanding" was upon Jesus. From a tender age he began to embody the wisdom of God (as he would later testify about himself, for example, *Luke 11:49*). This wisdom "that comes from heaven is first of all pure; then peace-loving, considerate, submissive, full of mercy and good fruit, impartial and sincere", wrote James, the brother of Jesus *(James 3:17)*. What better description of Jesus' own character could we offer than these words from his brother, Joseph's firstborn.

The "Spirit of counsel and of might" gave Jesus a plan of action and strength. The "Spirit of knowledge and fear of the Lord" equipped the young Jesus with the ability to distinguish between appearance and reality. It was a knowledge that went beyond the evidence of what he saw with his eyes or heard with his ears and became foundational for his interactions with others.

There are many other aspects of Isaiah's writings that pertain to this topic, but our primary focus here has been on the prophet's witness to the Messiah. The complete Old Testament picture is fuller still. From the initial messianic prophecy about the seed of the woman crushing the serpent's head *(Genesis 3:15)*, to the many other specific predictions scattered through the scriptures, must be added the broad sweep of Jewish history itself. Jesus fulfilled the royal ideal as Son of David *(Psalm 110; Matthew 22:41-45)* and Daniel's vision of the Son of Man *(Daniel 7:13ff)*. As prophet and lawgiver, he is greater than Moses *(cf. Matthew 5-7)*; as priest, he outranks Aaron *(Hebrews 5-7)*; as Servant of the Lord, he gives his life a ransom for many *(Mark 10:45)*. These and other strands of messianic prophecy were braided together by Jesus himself and reflect his consciousness of being God's Chosen and Anointed One. Such a consciousness was the fruit of the Spirit's work in his life, preparing the Son for his Father's instructed mission.

CHAPTER NINETEEN

Forces Visible and Invisible

It is the glory of God to conceal a matter; to search out a matter is the glory of kings.

Proverbs 25:2

We fix our eyes not on what is seen, but on what is unseen, since what is seen is temporary, but what is unseen is eternal.

2 Corinthians 4:18

Scientist Thomas Edison once pointed out that we do not know one-millionth of one per cent about anything. From the photosynthesis of the leaf to the beating of the heart, all nature is shot through with awe-provoking mystery. He reasoned that if science admits that the electron, the basis of all nature, is a complex affair, what of the Trinity, the author of the electron. In the twenty-first century our knowledge is greater, yet, at a fundamental level, all reality remains obscure. We know perhaps one per cent of one per cent of all that can be known. The very presence of mystery in the Bible, therefore, is evidence that it is dealing with, not avoiding, reality.

It is the same with the life of Christ: much is revealed, yet so much more concealed. Throughout the biblical narrative there are places when the curtain is pulled back and we glimpse a dimension of principalities and powers, unseen forces – angelic and demonic – that interact with our world (for example, see *Ephesians 6:12ff*). Perhaps unsurprisingly, we learn most about this from Jesus' life and teaching. Much remains hidden though, for example, about the interplay of spiritual forces before his public ministry, or the extent of the devil's knowledge about Jesus. Just as a veil of secrecy in the Old Testament surrounded Job's awareness of the forces arrayed against him, so our understanding concerning the spiritual dynamics of Christ's incarnation and upbringing remains clouded.

The New Testament has a great deal to say about the nature of the cosmic struggle humanity is embroiled in – specifically the demonic forces that were arrayed against Jesus during his lifetime. Was Satan aware of the significance of Jesus' coming to earth? We may wonder what he made of the dreams, visions, angelic appearances, and prophecies at the time of Jesus' birth? Perhaps the massacre of the boys two years and under in Bethlehem by King Herod was a satanically inspired attempt to remove Jesus before he could "destroy the devil's work" *(1 John 3:8)*. Apart from this episode, there is little to indicate Satan's presence until the temptations of Jesus. Might there have been other unreported attacks that took place during his early life that warranted special angelic protection?

Without the revelation of the Holy Spirit to illuminate scriptures such as messianic prophecies, perhaps Satan had much to work out concerning Jesus' identity and mission. For the principalities and powers he had come to disarm *(Colossians 2:15)*, it may have been the Father's intent for his Son to be spiritually incognito until his baptism – keeping those dark forces "second guessing" exactly what lay ahead. By speaking from heaven at the baptism *(Matthew 3:17)*, God was then, in effect, throwing down the gauntlet and proclaiming publicly to the spiritual forces of evil that the Son of God had come. The temptations that followed were spiritual warfare at its most intense; the stakes were high – the fate of humanity depended upon the outcome.

Jesus spoke with an authority and an urgency about the reality of spiritual warfare. Indeed, there is more recorded of his teaching about this than from anyone else in the Bible. He compared Satan to a marauding lord holding his possessions unchallenged until someone stronger came and cast him out *(Mark 3:22-26)*. Jesus knew he was locked in a critical conflict with dark powers, the "prince of this world" who had jurisdiction over human activity yet had "no hold" over Jesus *(John 14:30)*. Realising there would be ongoing conflict for his followers, even after the defeat of the devil by the work of the cross, Jesus taught them to pray, "Deliver us from the evil one" *(Matthew 6:13)*. This would be crucial, since in these "end times" Satan, in his death throes, continues to wreak havoc against all God's creation (see, for example, *Ephesians 6:12; 1 Peter 5:8*).

Jesus came to end the enemy occupation of the earth and take back the kingdom from "the strong man" *(Mark 3:27)*, so his encounter with Satan in the desert at the start of his ministry *(Matthew 4:1-11)* was unlikely to have been an initiation into cosmic spiritual conflict. Rather, he must have developed and established a deep understanding of this life-and-death struggle during his formative years. As already noted, "The reason the Son of God appeared was to destroy the devil's work" *(1 John 3:8)*. Jesus' growing self-awareness and consciousness of God's presence might have been paralleled by an increasing understanding of his enemy, even though we are not told exactly how his recognition of this dimension of evil came about.

Paul wrote to believers in Ephesus to help them understand and be better prepared for this spiritual battle. An adaptation of his message can help us appreciate that Jesus too needed to be fully equipped for battle – in fact, he is the perfect model and example for his followers:

> Throughout his life Jesus was strong in the Lord and in the strength of his might. He put on the armour of God and wore it in perfect obedience, so he might stand against the wiles of the devil. He, better than any, knew that his 'wrestling match' was not against enemies of blood and flesh – Roman or Jewish authorities – but against "the cosmic powers of this present darkness". This enabled him to stand on the evil day – and having done everything, to stand firm.

> From his earliest years he had worn the belt of truth, the breastplate of righteousness, the shoes of the gospel of peace. Together with these he took the shield of faith, the helmet of salvation, and the sword of the Spirit, which is the word of God. Yet on the cross, he freely divested himself of the armour that had perfectly protected him those 33 years. No principality or power forced him, but he chose to do this for our sake and for our salvation.

> *Based on Ephesians 6:10-17*

Matthew records three dreams that instructed, warned, and guided Joseph during the time of Jesus' birth and infancy *(Matthew 1:20, 2:9,13)*. Joseph's obedience to them was crucial in ensuring that God's purposes were fulfilled in Jesus. Our knowledge of their existence points to their impact upon Joseph. He considered them sufficiently important either to tell Matthew of them personally or to tell others, including, in all likelihood, Jesus himself. Was Jesus similarly directed and informed through divinely inspired dreams and visions? In *Psalm 16*, David says, in what is widely regarded as a messianic psalm, "I will praise the Lord, who counsels me; even at night my heart instructs me" *(Psalm 16:7)*.

The promise of the Spirit's coming upon human flesh, prophesied by Joel, was declared on the day of Pentecost by Peter *(Acts 2:17)*, but was fulfilled first by Jesus himself. God said:

> I will pour out my Spirit on all people.
> Your sons and daughters will prophesy,
> your old men will dream dreams,
> your young men will see visions.
> Even on my servants, both men and women,
> I will pour out my Spirit in those days.

Joel 2:28-29

Jesus as a young man may indeed have "seen visions", a characteristic of the age he was inaugurating. As a recipient of such "outpouring", this would certainly have impacted his early years.

Three times in the Gospels we read of the Father speaking audibly from heaven. Twice we read of angels coming to Jesus' aid: when he was being tempted in the desert and then again in Gethsemane. There is little reason to limit such occasions to his public ministry. The account of Jesus' transfiguration *(Matthew 17:1-9)* describes a spectacular event, but similar 'transfigurations', visions and supernatural manifestations might have happened earlier in his life. The biblical record is rich with accounts of those who encountered God's presence (for example, those mentioned in *Hebrews 11*). Paul, in a passage that may be autobiographical, described someone who...

> ...was caught up to the third heaven. Whether it was in the body or out of the body I do not know ... this man ... was caught up to paradise and heard inexpressible things, things that no-one is permitted to tell.

2 Corinthians 12:2-4

Again, we might ponder whether Jesus himself experienced similar marvels before his ministry.

The worldview which permeates much of our thinking in the Western world struggles to accept talk of angels and demons, invisible powers and the like because of the naturalistic assumptions and materialistic presuppositions prevalent today. Yet to be faithful to the biblical record we need to challenge these. If we fail to do so we will miss out on vital insights into Jesus' life and a dimension of reality from which we can learn so much.

CHAPTER TWENTY

Preparing for His Destiny

To move among the people on the common street; to meet
them in the market place on equal terms ... to bear the burdens
of society and relieve its needs; to carry on the multitudinous
activities of the city – in Christ's spirit and for his ends: this is
the religion of the Son of Man.

Henry Drummond

Jesus' mission is not laid out in its totality before him. He
cannot anticipate the content of the mission. The element of
prayer is thus necessary for Jesus. Every important event in
Jesus' life/mission involves prayer. It is in prayer to the Father
that his mission is communicated to him through the Holy
Spirit in stages which necessarily fit into the mission as a
whole.

Hans Urs von Balthasar

The New Testament begins with reference to Jesus as both the son of
David and son of Abraham *(Matthew 1:1-18)*. The reader is taken
through a synopsis of the Hebrew scriptures in the form of Jesus'
genealogical ancestry. The message is clear: if we want to know who Jesus
was and is, we must see him in the light of this story. He is the one who
fulfils the promises made to the Jewish people; he is the one who has
come among us to save us from our sins.

Jesus' ancestry has roots that draw upon ancient Israel's heroes of
faith as well as more dubious characters such as Rahab the prostitute
(Joshua 6:17). Luke takes us back to Adam and points to Jesus as a son
of man, *ben Adam*, and the son of God *(Luke 3:18)*. Joseph and Mary
would have shared their rich family legacy with Jesus (as they presumably
did with Matthew and Luke who both record his genealogy in their
Gospels from differing perspectives) and provided him with a treasure to
reflect on and cherish.

Perhaps from his meditations a seed was sown in Jesus' imagination to blossom in his later years in the name he gave himself: Son of Man. He may first have come across the phrase while reading Psalm 8 and found himself sharing the writer's sense of awe, reflecting on his own identity.

> What is mankind that you are mindful of them, human beings [lit. 'Son of Man'] that you care for them? You have made them a little lower than the angels and crowned him with glory and honor. You made them rulers over the works of your hands; you put everything under their feet.
>
> *Psalm 8:4-6*

As a boy, Jesus was only too conscious of his humanity – he was a normal teenager growing up in a carpenter's family in Nazareth, an ordinary "son of man". But he was more than a mere descendant of Adam. His parents, the prophecies, and the witness of the Spirit told him so. We can wonder at what Jesus must have felt reading Daniel's description of the "son of man" who approached God, the "Ancient of Days", and represented his people before the throne:

> In my vision at night I looked, and there before me was one like a son of man, coming with the clouds of heaven. He approached the Ancient of Days and was led into his presence. He was given authority, glory and sovereign power; all nations and peoples of every language worshipped him. His dominion is an everlasting dominion that will not pass away, and his kingdom is one that will never be destroyed.
>
> *Daniel 7:13-14*

In searching the scriptures for clarity about his own identity, Jesus would have come across passages such as this. It must have been breathtaking as the Spirit pointed out to Jesus that these verses referred to him; he was central to God's purposes here on earth.

Colloquially we speak about 'light bulb' moments, or that time when 'the penny drops' and something suddenly becomes clear and makes sense. There must have been many such moments for Jesus. He chose Son of Man as a title for himself, a one-phrase parable, so to speak, which was able to simultaneously *reveal* and *conceal* his true nature. Those responsive to God would see in him this "son of man" Daniel foretold. Those unwilling to become disciples would see in him only a son of man, a frail descendant of Adam who, like them, was subject to death. Just as the parables were riddles that revealed or obscured truth, depending on the heart disposition of the hearer, so 'Son of Man' was a term that perfectly embraced his identity and described his destiny: his humanity as suffering Servant of the Lord and his deity as victorious King.

Listening to a rabbi in the synagogue, or to his parents at home, as a pupil in school or in his private reading, Jesus must have had many opportunities to discover the truth about his identity that he would later use to challenge the religious leaders:

> Do not think I will accuse you before the Father. Your accuser is Moses, on whom your hopes are set. If you believed Moses, you would believe me, for he wrote about me. But since you do not believe what he wrote, how are you going to believe what I say?

> *John 5:45-47*

Jesus lived in the light of the ongoing, progressive revelation he was receiving. The broad outline of what lay ahead was being revealed to him; specific details, in all likelihood, were not. He may well not have known all the answers or understood everything as he faced the uncertainties and ambiguities of life and the unpredictable responses of others. Yet the reality of the statement in Proverbs may also have been applicable:

> The path of the righteous is like the morning sun, shining ever brighter till the full light of day.

> *Proverbs 4:18*

Nevertheless, as Habakkuk prophesied, "My righteous one shall live by faith" *(Habakkuk 2:4; Hebrews 10:38)* and faith was as necessary to Jesus' walk as to ours. Jesus, the pioneer of faith *(Hebrews 12:2)*, faced every situation with a response of faith-filled trust and obedience, and through this discerned the Father's perspective and what he was saying.

Like the ancients, Jesus had God's approval through his faith *(Hebrews 10:39, 11:6)*. His insights into his heavenly identity as Messiah and Emmanuel (God with us, *Matthew 1:23*) probably came gradually – like the first gleam of dawn – although there may also have been additional times of revelation at various decisive points in his upbringing. We have seen that from Jesus' earliest glimmers of insight as a child to the radiant confidence he demonstrated as an adult in the Gospels, divine and human factors were woven together. There was the witness of the

Spirit to his spirit, which corroborated the witness of the Father. This was enriched and clarified by the scriptures Jesus studied. There were the individuals God used, such as his parents who told him of their own experience of angels and dreams. They could also share what they had heard from others: shepherds, wise men, Simeon, Anna, Zechariah, and Elizabeth. Each was sent by God to bear witness to this truth.

In our quest to discover more of Jesus' background, we have on occasion applied teaching from the New Testament epistles to Jesus' own life. Since he is the author and perfecter of our faith *(Hebrews 2:10, 12:2)*, he is our pattern and prototype, and therefore exhortations addressed to us can be related back to Jesus' own experience. This can help us, for example, understand Jesus' own struggle against sin. The apostle Paul described his intense personal struggle to overcome sinful tendencies and habits in his letter to Christians in Rome *(Romans 7)*. While interpreters disagree over whether or not he is describing his experience before becoming a Christian, what is clear from the following chapter is his encounter with the Spirit's power in his life to conquer sin.

To consider the nature of the battle for Jesus, we can apply these New Testament teachings. He came "in the likeness of sinful flesh" *(Romans 8:3)*, thus "shared in their humanity" *(Hebrews 2:14)*, and "...has been tempted in every way, just as we are – yet he did not sin" *(Hebrews 4:15)*. Let us reflect on how Jesus' struggle may have both differed from, and been similar to, our own. Adapting a further section of Paul's letter to the Romans and applying it to Jesus may help us understand his experience.

> There could be no condemnation for Jesus; throughout his life the law of the Spirit of life continually set him free from the law of sin and death. (The Law of Moses was powerless to do this because it was weakened by man's sinful nature, but the Father, by sending his own Son in the likeness of sinful man to be a sin offering, condemned sin in sinful man.) The righteous requirements of the law were fully met in Jesus who, from his earliest days, refused to live according to man's sinful nature and yielded himself continually to the Spirit.

> He lived in accordance with the Spirit and set his mind on what the Spirit desired. By contrast with others, Jesus' mind was continually controlled by the Spirit and so he enjoyed life and peace. The mind of Jesus was not hostile to God because

he submitted himself to God's law. (Those controlled by their sinful nature cannot please God, but Jesus was not controlled by a sinful nature, but by the Spirit, because the Spirit of God lived in him and he always pleased his Father.)

By the Spirit, Jesus repeatedly put to death the misdeeds of the body and lived – really lived. As the Son of God, he was always led by the Spirit of God. He had not received a spirit that made him a slave living in fear. He had the Spirit of sonship and cried out, "Abba, Father!" The Spirit himself testified with his spirit that he was God's child. Because he was the child of God he knew he was also the heir of God. (He later suffered in order to share in his Father's glory and did not consider this suffering worth comparing with the glory that was to be revealed to him.)

Based on Romans 8:1-21

Jesus is our inspiration. He continually made right choices; he could have sinned but chose not to. This not only set him apart from everyone who has ever lived, but it can inspire us to depend on the Spirit as he did.

By way of further illustration, here are other examples of adapting material addressed to believers that can help us better understand Jesus as an individual facing experiences similar to our own. They are equally applicable to the final 1,000 days of his ministry, as to the preceding 10,000 days.

What we are instructed to do, Christ did first.

In Gethsemane on the night before his crucifixion, at his baptism and on countless previous occasions...

Jesus presented his body as a living sacrifice, holy and acceptable to God. Rather than be conformed to this world, he allowed his mind to be transformed so that he discerned the will of his Father – what is good, acceptable, and perfect.

Based on Romans 12:1-2

By intentional exercise of his will, Jesus consistently made wise choices. We glean further insights by adapting a portion of Paul's letter to the Philippian Christians:

Jesus was not anxious about anything, but in everything, by prayer and petition, with thanksgiving, he presented his requests to God. And the peace of God, which transcends all understanding, guarded his heart and his mind. Whatever is true, whatever is noble, whatever is right, whatever is pure, whatever is lovely, whatever is admirable – if anything is excellent or praiseworthy – Jesus thought about such things.

Based on Philippians 4:6-8

We are to receive insight from God in a similar way to Jesus.

Things which eye has not seen and ear has not heard and which have not entered the heart of man, all this God prepared for the Son who loved him. These things were revealed to him through the Spirit; for the Spirit searches all things – even the depths of God. Jesus knew the thoughts of God because he had not received the spirit of the world, but the Spirit who is from God, so that he might know the things freely given to him by God. Jesus spoke about these things, not in words taught by human wisdom, but in those taught by the Spirit, combining spiritual thoughts with spiritual words. These words were spiritually appraised by him who, because he was spiritual, appraised all things, yet was himself not appraised by anyone.

Based on 1 Corinthians 2:9-15

That which distinguishes a true Christian from others first distinguished Christ.

Jesus' love was genuine; he hated what was evil and held fast to what is good. He loved others with genuine affection, showing honour to others. He was not lagging in zeal, was ardent in spirit, and served the Lord. He rejoiced in hope, was patient in suffering, and persevered in prayer.

Based on Romans 12:9-12

The struggles we experience as believers, Christ also experienced.

Jesus exalted in his tribulations, knowing that tribulation brings about perseverance; perseverance, proven character; proven character, hope; and hope did not disappoint him, because the love of God had been poured out within his heart through the Holy Spirit who had been given him.

Based on Romans 5:2-5

156

The character of Jesus shines through such passages when read in the light of all that he went through. Jesus testified at his trial before Pilate:

> "In fact, the reason I was born and came into the world is to testify to the truth. Everyone on the side of truth listens to me."

John 18:37

His understanding was by now so complete that he claimed to be "the Way, the Truth and the Life" *(John 14:6)*. We have traced the different influences that gave rise to the fullness of the revelation he has provided us with in his teaching – from his initial awareness of his unique identity and role which reached its zenith as he prepared himself to reveal these awe-inspiring truths to others.

Chapter Twenty-One

Sermon from Life

The busier life is, the more need there is for a still center, a place deep within us to which we can withdraw after the day-to-day buffeting and storms: a place where we can mull over events and savor them more fully, a place where above all, we can listen ... to what God is saying through circumstances, through people, through creation and his word spoken in the depth of our being.

Sister Margaret Magdalen

The glory of God is seen in a human life lived to the full.[138]

Irenæus of Lyons

There comes a special moment in everyone's life, a moment for which that person was born. That special opportunity, when he seizes it, will fulfil his mission – a mission for which he is uniquely qualified. In that moment, he finds greatness. It is his finest hour.

Winston Churchill

Here is a man, sinless, because he has lovingly allowed the Father's will full scope in his life. Here is a man with an utterly free interior life, under the most restricted and oppressive conditions, simply through prayer; as we see from the sovereign self-consciousness he displays in dialogue with his disciples and, even more, with his enemies. Here is a man whose love is perfect, although he often makes of others the same inflexible demands he makes of himself.

Here is the complete man; not a man who fits in with all and sundry, but a strong and distinctive personality, utterly

---

[138] Irenaeus, *Against Heresies* Book 4, chapter 34 section 7

unforgettable, whose words and deeds are unique and inimitable, whose influence on history is supreme. The perfect friend, the perfect leader, whose energy, however concentrated, never distorted his character, who always remained fresh and even childlike, with no false sophistication, loving children (a sure sign!) and commending their outlook on life to those who liked to think themselves "adult." He never reacts in a banal, predictable way; all that he does is original and creative.[139]

Hans Urs von Balthasar

We can learn a great deal about Jesus' early life from the teaching he gave during his public ministry. The Sermon on the Mount *(Matthew 5-7)*, arguably the most important speech ever given, provides insights into Jesus' own personal character, shaped over many years. It reveals:

- his motives (for example, the intent is as important as the deed, *5:21-48*)
- his attitudes (for example, poor in spirit, merciful, pure in heart, *5:3-11*)
- his priorities (for example, seek first the kingdom of God, *6:33*)

Here is the expression of a life fully yielded to God over three decades that would be perfectly demonstrated over the next three years. Jesus' teaching reflected his own discipleship – his motives, attitudes, and priorities. Words he addressed to others, he had first applied to his own life. The Father, his Rabbi, had perfectly trained him *(John 12:49)*, so he could proclaim, "Anyone who has seen me has seen the Father" *(John 14:9)*. God's character was displayed in the instructions Jesus taught and the way he gave them.

Jesus began with the beatitudes, or "beautiful attitudes" as they have been called, which mirror his own approach to life. It could be said that Jesus 'clothed himself' with the beatitudes; not suddenly becoming "poor in spirit", "merciful" or "hungering and thirsting for righteousness" at the outset of his preaching. No, these qualities sum up how he had already lived, and who he had become at that point. To these attributes he attached promises; assurances of blessing, once whispered by the Father to him, now extended to others:

[139] Hans Urs von Balthasar, *Prayer Part II, The Word is Made Flesh*

159

Blessed are the poor in spirit, for theirs is the kingdom of heaven.
Blessed are those who mourn, for they will be comforted.
Blessed are the meek, for they will inherit the earth.
Blessed are those who hunger and thirst for righteousness, for they will be filled.
Blessed are the merciful, for they will be shown mercy.
Blessed are the pure in heart, for they will see God.
Blessed are the peacemakers, for they will be called children of God.
Blessed are those who are persecuted because of righteousness, for theirs is the kingdom of heaven.

Matthew 5:3-10

Jesus interacted with the spiritual thinking of his culture; so while his statements are recognised as central to his teaching, they can also be matched by quotations from the Talmud (the oral tradition that was passed down among the rabbis). A study of the Gospels reveals many such examples of rabbinic influence, in content, phraseology, and argumentation. Through this we have a glimpse into Jesus' mind during the closing 'hidden' years of preparation before his ministry. While fully aware of contemporary Jewish thought, he added his own distinctive imprint by refashioning it according to his personal walk with God.

Jesus expressed himself in a rabbinical style, using parable *(mashal)* and commentary *(derasha)* to expound fundamental Jewish concepts. A distinctive about his teaching was not so much his references to scripture or his language; it was his bold self-expression, independence, and initiative – interpreted by the Pharisees as arrogance, and at times blasphemy. He spoke authoritatively in God's Name, not through the traditions of the rabbis, but as one who had a personal relationship with God. He knew what he was talking about.

Nestled in the heart of the Sermon on the Mount is the prayer that Jesus taught his disciples *(Matthew 6:9-13)*. It may owe its origin in part to one Jesus would have used at a time of personal loss. For, as the eldest child, Jesus would have been called upon to pray at the family tomb on his father's death and may well have recited an ancient prayer, the *kaddish*, still said by Jewish orphans today. He may have prayed it again soon after, in the synagogue, when publicly lamenting his father's absence. The Jewish prayer has some similarities of expression and content with the prayer Jesus taught his disciples.

> Magnified and great be his great name in the world which he has created according to his will. May he establish his kingdom during your life and during your days ... Let his great name be blessed forever and to all eternity. Blessed, praised and glorified, exalted, extolled and honoured, magnified and lauded be the name of the Holy One, blessed be he ... He who makes peace in his high places, may he make peace for us and for all Israel; and say you, Amen.

Probing deeper, it seems the prayer Jesus taught his disciples was born out of his own understanding and experience. It can therefore provide us with further clues into his developing awareness of identity and purpose – who he was and why he had come to earth. Each phrase seems to represent a distillation of his life's observations, to be reflected back to God in prayer. Let's consider each phrase in turn.

- *Our Father in heaven*
  As we have already noted, from earliest childhood Jesus called upon *Abba*, 'my Father'. Before he was 12 he was aware Joseph was not his earthly father and was already devoting his life to cultivating a relationship with his Father in heaven. From that would come the unfolding and, perhaps sometimes, overwhelming revelation of his true identity and life's purpose. This would be confirmed through open communication with the one he instinctively called *Abba*, a relationship nurtured by his earthly parents as they too developed in comprehension of their son's uniqueness.
- *Hallowed be your name*
  As his awareness of Father and Spirit increased, Jesus would have inevitably experienced a sense of being different from others, which may have led to feelings of isolation and even loneliness. However, the greater compensation of God's presence gave Jesus a serenity and peace that we see portrayed by the Gospel writers. Combined with that, though, was his awareness that in the prevailing culture his Father's holiness was not fully appreciated by many. Religious groups often failed to understand and explain God's true character. This was therefore

161

a heartfelt cry, from Jesus and communicated to his disciples, that all should know and appreciate the Father as he himself did.

- *Your kingdom come, your will be done, on earth as it is in heaven*
  Growing up, Jesus inevitably witnessed sickness, death, injustice, social tension, mistrust… and must have developed a deep longing for wrongs to be righted, for justice to prevail, for God's rule to be established. His passion was for transformation and new creation, for the Father to intervene – an apocalyptic event that would usher in a new kingdom rule on earth and eliminate all that opposed God's will and purposes.

- *Give us today our daily bread*
  Amidst the harsh economic climate with poverty and deprivation on every side, Jesus longed for God's provision to be shared among the needy. This was an intensely practical request, perhaps born out of financial struggles his own family would have had to endure.

- *Forgive us our debts as we also have forgiven our debtors*
  Jesus was acutely conscious of the fallenness of society, with its corrupt institutions and broken individuals. Although he himself had done no wrong, his prayer on behalf of others was as passionate as if seeking forgiveness for his own shortcomings. He may 'owe' nothing himself, but he carried the concerns of others' 'debts' before God, and our need to have a forgiving attitude towards any who have wronged us.

- *And lead us not into temptation, but deliver us from the evil one*
  Behind the brokenness surrounding him, Jesus discerned the identity of malevolent powers intent on defacing the image of God in humankind and perverting his intentions for creation. A fervency of spirit towards evil and everything opposed to his Father rose within him, and a determination to do all that was necessary to resist and overcome evil forces. This was a passionate cry for people to be set free from the grip of a powerful enemy.

With these foundational insights in place, Jesus knew the appointed time had come for him to begin his mission; his identity, his calling, and his destiny were assured.

Jesus' teaching made evident his fulfilment and delight in his heavenly Father; the pleasure in this special relationship matched only by the joy of it being reciprocated. *Abba* was the source of his self-confidence, his authority, and his humility, and the enjoyment of their mutual love was the foundation for Jesus' strength *(Nehemiah 8:10)*, energising him to resist temptation and pursue the "narrow way" that leads to life *(Matthew 7:13)*. It caused him to take the lonely road to the cross and "taste death for everyone" *(Hebrews 2:9)*, thereby demonstrating that "the God who is spirit is also love. God's essence is spirit – God's character is love."[140] Never was God's love more clearly shown than in the words and deeds of his Son.

As Jesus' self-knowledge grew, so did his knowledge of the Father's love for him and others. This he lived out, and taught others to do the same in what is often known as the Golden Rule: "In everything, do to others what you would have them do to you, for this sums up the Law and the Prophets" *(Matthew 7:12)*. Without a robust understanding of the Father's love, the identity, calling, and destiny of the Son would have made no sense; for this was the source and explanation for all three. Jesus would offer his body as a living sacrifice that was holy and pleasing to God; this was his spiritual act of worship *(cf. Romans 12:1)*.

> He, like us, was made of frail human flesh, in order to expel sin from human flesh. He came to invite us to become like himself, commissioning us to imitate God, placing us under obedience to the Father so that we might see and know God. He who did this is the Word of God, who lived in and became Son of humankind in order to accustom humans to live in God and to accustom God to live in humanity.
>
> *Irenæus*

---

140 Clark Pinnock, *Flame of Love,* 29

CHAPTER TWENTY-TWO

A Heart on Fire

In the high hills around his home Jesus the workman slowly dreamed into objective form the message he had been born to deliver. Now his heart was on fire with a dangerous purpose...[141]

Fulton Oursler

The silent power of a consistent life.

Florence Nightingale

He came to save all through his own person; all, that is, who through him are reborn to God; infants, children, boys, young men and old. Therefore he passed through every stage of life. He was made an infant for infants, sanctifying infancy; a child among children, sanctifying childhood, and setting an example of filial affection. Of righteousness and of obedience, a young man among young men, becoming an example to them and sanctifying them to the Lord. So also he was a grown man among the older men, that he might be a perfect teacher for all, not merely in respect to revelation of the truth, but also in respect of this stage of life, sanctifying the older men, and becoming an example to them also.

Irenæus

If there is any truth to the adage that "the boy is the father of the man", then we have to conclude that the youthful Jesus must have been developing an extraordinary sense of mission, of a call toward something other than his work-a-day life as an inhabitant of a small provincial town. But what that vocation was remained to be seen. By the time he was 30 years

---

[141] Fulton Oursler, *The Greatest Story Ever Told*

of age or thereabouts, the urgency became clear. He must strike out on his own to the Jordan where John was baptizing and calling for a spiritual renewal among the chosen people.

Richard W. Kropf

Contrary to what some theologians have proposed, I would argue that the idea of Jesus as the Christ, the Son of God, did not originate with the early church but with Jesus himself. This was how he understood himself and what he communicated to his disciples.

Australian theologian Paul Barnett proposes that Jesus' awareness of his identity and relationship with God arose from four quarters.[142] First, that Joseph taught his son about his Davidic descent; second, Jesus read the scriptures through the eyes of that long-awaited son of David; third, the preaching of John the Baptist established this was God's appointed hour; and finally, when Jesus was baptised by John in the Jordan, God's voice affirmed to Jesus that he was indeed God's Son. However, as has been seen, this is too cautious an analysis, for it downplays the decisive role played by the Holy Spirit in Jesus' life. It has therefore been suggested in our exploration that the Spirit used the Jewish culture and Jesus' own family to steer his understanding and help him interpret his destiny – human and divine – long before John's preaching and baptism.

"Didn't you know I had to be in my Father's house?" said the twelve-year-old Jesus to his parents. It could be said that these words not only applied to that original incident in the Temple *(Luke 2:41-50)* but also became the defining quality of Jesus' life from that moment. As Steve Anderson maintains:

> In all the hidden years of his childhood, our Lord was doing the work of his Father in Heaven and being about his business ... whether in the carpenter's shop or in the marketplace, whether at home or travelling on the road, whether in glorious Jerusalem, in the busy streets of Nazareth or in the obscurity of Bethlehem, the Lord Jesus was at all times doing the will of his Father. Perfect and consistent, he was being and doing exactly what he should have been doing in order to please his Father.

---

[142] Paul Barnett, *Jesus & the Rise of Early Christianity: A History of New Testament Times*, 34

At the outset of this investigation, the two parts of Jesus' life were likened to a long-jump, where an extended period of preparation – the run-up – is followed by the jump itself. Jesus' baptism and temptation finally confirmed and tested the completeness of his 10,000 days of training; everything necessary had been accomplished for him to embark on his 'jump' into 1,000 days of public ministry. By then Jesus knew exactly who he was, what he should tell others, and why he had come to earth. The Father affirmed his total commitment and devotion to his Son in the pronouncement, "This is my Son whom I love; with him I am well pleased" *(Matthew 3:17; Luke 3:21-23)*. The Message translation elaborates: "This is my son, chosen and marked by my love, delight of my life." The declaration, rich with significance, echoed three important Old Testament passages that Jesus would have recognised as applying to himself: *Genesis 22:1-11, Isaiah 42:1,* and *Psalm 2:7.* As has been shown, each highlight complementary aspects of who Jesus was and what he had come to do; each contained a foreshadowing of the Messiah.

As already observed, *Genesis 22* recalls Abraham's obedience in offering Isaac, his "only son, the one he loved". On the mount of the Lord, God would provide the lamb for the sacrifice. Isaiah speaks of God's servant, the one who fulfils the longings of a nation: "Here is my servant, whom I uphold, my chosen in whom I delight!" *(Isaiah 42:1, cf. 49:3)*. Jesus was that Servant who would suffer rejection, humiliation, and death *(Isaiah 52:11-53:12)*. He would not only enable Israel to fulfil its destiny as a light to the nations, as Christ, the Light of the World, Jesus would usher in a new era *(John 8:12)*. In the Psalms, David speaks prophetically of the Lord who has installed his king on Zion. The Anointed One says, "I will proclaim the Lord's decree: He said to me, 'You are my Son; today I have become your Father.'" *(Psalm 2:7)*.

Together such scriptures affirmed the revelation Jesus had received in the preceding years about his identity, calling, and mission. The Father's words from heaven at his baptism were full of reassurance, affirmation, inspiration, and challenge – so crucial for Jesus that Satan directly contested this in the wilderness soon after, taunting, "If you are the Son of God..." In other words, "Can you really believe what God said?"

The hidden years over, the panorama of the New Testament story now came into full view. Having lived unnoticed for the past three decades, Jesus emerged into the full blaze of public attention. What happened during the following three years would make him the pivot of history, so much so that years would be calculated from his presumed date of birth. Though secret to the world, Jesus' first 10,000 days were lived in the presence of the Father who was preparing him for the work of redemption. This time was no less a period of service than afterwards when the public spotlight was upon him. For 30 years his character had been fashioned; he was "gentle and humble in heart" *(Matthew 11:29)*, as U.S. President John Adams put it, "Jesus is benevolence personified, an example to all."

The fruit of the Spirit describes Jesus' character perfectly *(Galatians 5:22-23)*: he was full of love, joy, peace, patience, kindness, goodness, faithfulness, gentleness, and self-control. Anointed with the Holy Spirit, the gifts of the Spirit describe his power *(1 Corinthians 12:8-11)*; and the ministry-gifts to the Church describe his authority: as apostle, prophet, evangelist, shepherd, and teacher *(Ephesians 4:11)*. These qualities and attributes were developed throughout many years of instruction and discipleship.

During the next 1,000 days, God's character, authority, and power were seen in Jesus in an unparalleled and unprecedented way. After years of hearing his Father misrepresented, Jesus could at last declare what he was really like. He did so with a passion, urgency, and confidence that astounded those who heard him. When Jesus met a leper *(Matthew 8:1-4)*, for example, we sense his relief and joy. Finally, he could say, "I am willing; be clean!" After years of seeing leprosy sufferers shunned and despised, now at last he could demonstrate God's kingdom and his love for such people. It appears that Jesus had a joyful as well as a compassionate spirit. If he had been a gloomy Messiah, he would hardly have attracted children, the depressed, and the sick in the way he did.

Jesus lived perfectly as Servant and King: one who was of earth and also of heaven. During those ministry years, many came to observe his steadfastness of purpose in keeping to the appointed task. There was simplicity, self-discipline, and a serenity of spirit about him that attracted others to him like a magnet. His life was characterised by strong gentleness: "He will not quarrel or cry out; no one will hear his voice in the streets. A bruised reed he will not break, and a smouldering wick he will not snuff out," wrote Matthew, quoting the prophet Isaiah *(Matthew 12:19-20)*.

As one made "like his brothers", a son of Adam, Jesus undoubtedly felt, and sometimes expressed, a variety of emotions; yet he always maintained self-control. The Son of God experienced success but without pride; adverse circumstances without bitterness; temptation without yielding to its pressure. If any moment of his life could be frozen in time, there would be nothing worthy of regret or criticism. Albert Einstein, an agnostic, observed that "no objective reader could read the Gospels without feeling the actual presence of Jesus. His personality pulsates in every word. No myth is filled with such life."[143]

The Gospels reveal Jesus as a man of prayer. The disciples' request, "Lord, teach us to pray" *(Luke 11:1)*, came as they observed the unique nature of Jesus' prayer life. When we read of Jesus interceding, meditating, weeping in prayer for others, we glimpse the life of someone who treasured and nurtured communion with *Abba*, his Father, above all else. His greatest and most complete prayer was uttered in the words "Your will be done" – called the "pure prayer of love" by former Archbishop of Canterbury Rowan Williams. Not only was it prayed in final agony at the culmination of his life, this had been a ceaseless aspiration since his earliest days.

Jesus' realisation of himself as the Messiah had grown out of an intimate relationship between his Father, the Spirit, and him; and from this had flowed an understanding of his role (see *Luke 4:14-21* for his manifesto). Receiving this revelation was not just an intellectual exercise for Jesus, rather it came more as a developing child learns and increases in awareness – quietly, steadily, experientially.

Each of Jesus' references to children seems in part autobiographical. As he had sensed his Father's pleasure and delight from an early age, he could later state that "the kingdom of God belongs to such as these" *(Mark 10:14)*. Having discerned as a child the angelic presence and protection over his life he could say, "...their angels in heaven always see the face of my Father in heaven" *(Matthew 18:10)*. From his earliest years Jesus had approached his Father with humility, trust, and love. He had embraced the kingdom with the enthusiasm of a child receiving a gift, so it was natural to declare, "...whoever takes the lowly position of this child is the greatest in the kingdom of heaven" *(Matthew 18:4)*.

Jesus' child-like trust enabled him to live with questions for which he may not yet have had answers, and a peace that guarded his mind where others would have worried. This child-like spirit grew out of a daily dependence upon *Abba*, his Father, from earliest years. Jesus taught his followers about living free from anxiety and not having concerns for material things *(Matthew 6)*, showing that he wanted them to trust their

---

[143] Walter Isaacson, *Einstein and Faith* (*Time* 169, April 5), 47

heavenly Father too, and enjoy the carefree abandonment that he himself experienced.

Jesus spoke authoritatively to adults of their need to change: "…unless you change and become like little children…" *(Matthew 18:3)*. He was stern to those who mistreated children, saying, "See that you do not despise one of these little ones" *(Matthew 18:10)*. His own memories formed the backdrop for remarks to adults about children and he used his personal recollections of boyhood to model how they should be treated.

The Gospels set out Jesus' teaching and miracles during those last 1,000 days on earth and give unique clues into insights he had previously acquired. "The mouth speaks what the heart is full of" *(Matthew 12:34)* applies as much to his own words as to those he was addressing. What he taught flowed from who he was and what he had experienced prior to his ministry. The qualities so apparent in Jesus as an adult grew from "mustard seed" beginnings in infancy to their fullest expression in his manhood. Jesus must have been an astute and sensitive observer of others and of life around him as a young person, for we read of his extraordinary powers of perception as an adult.

We can imagine the dry, legalistic teaching preached in the synagogues that Jesus had listened to year after year, and the hypocrisy he often saw in the religious leaders. Now his "time had come" and he could speak out, warning his disciples against such things in the Sermon on the Mount *(Matthew 5-7)*. We can imagine the joy he sensed whenever he saw the faith of God-fearing men and women and their lives of humble obedience. After years of preparation, the Father told him that the time was right and the greatest storyteller the world has seen at last had permission to speak out truths he had longed to impart.

Jesus brought truth to life by using ordinary, understandable images. By one reckoning the Gospels record 18 major stories by Jesus, approximately 60 analogies, and, in John's Gospel, 16 metaphors. Jesus' favourite form of speech was the parable. Of the 40 or so parables in the synoptic Gospels, only a couple mention God by name, yet these simple stories had a subversive quality precisely because they sounded so ordinary and secular. Jesus' parables were about farmers and merchants, bandits and victims, soil and seeds, meals, coins, sheep, and everyday observations of life in that culture.

Through the vivid imagery of the parables, we see the world through Jesus' eyes. We catch a glimpse of his Nazareth home at night: "No-one lights a lamp and puts it in a place where it will be hidden..." *(Luke 11:33)*; "My yoke is easy and my burden is light" *(Matthew 11:30)*. His listeners could easily imagine the familiar sight of oxen toiling under the weight of the plough. There are references to birds, snakes, foxes, and wolves; stories of swineherds and pigs, sowers of seed, and weeds in the wheat fields, lost sheep, good and bad shepherds; all these things reflect the rural surroundings of Jesus and his hearers. There are parables of judges, courtiers, poor tenants, and rich landowners – people of various walks of life, seen in towns and cities across the land.

Paul Barnett, commenting on one story, writes:

> The Parable of the Pounds is really an historical allegory based on Archelaus' visit to Rome in 4BC – more than 30 years earlier – to take possession of his father Herod's kingdom. It reveals Jesus' awareness of politics and of recent history. When at last he opens his mouth to speak, the vivid imagery he uses conveys something of the impact on him of the things he saw in those intervening years.

When people heard Jesus tell such stories they did not immediately equate the truths with their own religious experiences. Instead they relaxed their defences, listened intently and went away pondering this new teacher's words. But the stories lodged in their imagination, to come to life later. Only then did they realise the impact of truth – Jesus was talking about God and his kingdom. They had been invaded!

CHAPTER TWENTY-THREE

A New Humanity

Let our chief endeavor be to meditate on the life of Jesus Christ.

Thomas à Kempis

When you read God's word you must constantly be saying to yourself, "It is talking to me, and about me." [144]

Soren Kierkegaard

The Lord desires to be loved and taken seriously as man too; as a man, he wants to inspire men and – why not? – arouse their enthusiastic discipleship.

Hans Urs von Balthasar

For this he assumed my body, that I may become capable of his Word; taking my flesh, he gives me his spirit; and so, he bestowing and I receiving, he prepares for me the treasure of Life. He takes my flesh, to sanctify me; he gives me his Spirit that he may save me.

John Chrysostom

Jesus' human story is inseparable and incomprehensible without seeing it also as a story of the Holy Spirit. That story is a prophetic prototype of the Spirit's story with us. The Christian's story is a story of the Spirit partially paralleling the unique story of Jesus. It is by the Spirit we are regenerated and born again. By the Spirit we are anointed to serve and extend the kingdom. By the Spirit we will be brought through death and raised to glorious life. [145]

Simon Ponsonby

---

[144] Soren Kierkegaard, *For Self-Examination*
[145] Ponsonby, *God Inside Out*, 27

As our exploration draws to a close, let us consider once more the radical decision of the Trinity in instigating the miracle of incarnation, and how this has become the prototype for a new relationship between God and those who follow him. The journey of discovery Jesus that took into an awareness of his own identity, calling, and destiny becomes the pattern for all Christians down through the ages. Through the energising presence of the Father and the Spirit and the revelation of God's word, the same resources available to Jesus are also offered to his followers. So, too, that same humble, submissive dependence that Jesus demonstrated perfectly in his life on earth is required by believers.

To underline a key verse, in the letter to the Hebrews we read of God's promise to his Son: "You are my Son; today I have become your Father ... I will be his Father; and he will be my Son" *(Hebrews 1:5).* While this verse has its roots firmly in the Old Testament, reflecting historic references to Davidic kingship, the writer also looks beyond these, seeing they are but a shadow of a greater reality. For "when the set time had fully come" *(Galatians 4:4),* God became Father to the human Jesus. A dynamic parent-child relationship was inaugurated as God's only Son became human through the mystery and miracle of the incarnation.

Whether or not the Son is eternally subordinated to the Father is a matter of considerable debate among theologians but on balance it seems as if the eternal mutual self-submission of the persons of the Trinity shifted to encompass a new reality. Henceforth, because of his human status with its increased vulnerability and needs, the Son would be in submission to God, his heavenly Father. For the duration of Jesus' earthly pilgrimage, his relationship with God the Father would no longer be one of mutual submission, as previously. The most fitting description for this new relationship is that of a parent with his child; the Son joyfully submitting to the Father, taking instructions from him and following his initiative.

A father's love and care produces a special bond, altruistic and committed, also protective and concerned for the other's well-being and development. With no biological human father, and because of his unique identity, calling, and destiny, Jesus would face challenges and privileges far greater than those of any other child. For this reason, the Creator God is described as assuming a parental role, declaring, "I will be a father to him; he will be my son." Prefigured and prophesied in the Hebrew scriptures, this new way of interacting, brought about by the vulnerability and dependency of Jesus' circumstances, meant this father-son language was particularly apt. Jesus' need was now for a protector, provider, guardian, instructor – as never before.

The Gospels show us that Jesus delighted in his role as Son (for example, *Matthew 11:25-27*), so much so that his passion was to share this with his followers and invite them into the special relationship. Thus God would be "everlasting father" to his children *(cf. Isaiah 9:6)*. And we too can now pray with confidence to "our Father" *(Matthew 6:9)*. The need for God's protection and provision by Jesus' followers differs from his only in the significance of his role over theirs.

The Spirit as *Paraclete* or Helper *(John 14:26)* echoes the description of Eve for Adam as a "helper suitable for him" *(Genesis 2:20)*. For the Spirit was Jesus' constant companion and mentor in a way not experienced before the incarnation. As the Spirit had hovered over creation *(Genesis 1:2)* so now the Spirit brooded over the new creation of the God-Man.

The divine parenting Jesus experienced from conception to ascension has become the prototype and pattern for the loving provision God has for each of his children *(2 Corinthians 6:18)*. Jesus experienced this in two ways: as it was expressed through Joseph and Mary, insofar as they were sensitive to obey the promptings of the Spirit in their interactions with Jesus, and as it was mediated directly to Jesus' mind and spirit by the Holy Spirit.

Since "whoever is united with the Lord is one with him in spirit" *(1 Corinthians 6:17)* it can be assumed that the Father and the Spirit ministered to the deepest level of Jesus' being. As we have noted, "the Spirit searches all things, even the deep things of God" *(1 Corinthians 2:10)*. As a tiny baby this might have been simply as a warm or comforting presence, an atmosphere of calmness – *Shalom*. From these first impressions, the Spirit would go on to bear witness to Jesus' spirit that he was indeed not merely "a child of God" but *the* Child of God *(Romans 8:16)*.

As Jesus' understanding grew as a child, the content would have become more informative; and there would also have been a strong moral element to this as his "conscience confirmed it through the Holy Spirit" *(cf. Romans 9:1)*. At every stage, we can imagine the Father and Spirit in partnership to ensure the young Jesus received what was necessary to bring clarity and wisdom. In this, Jesus was an active recipient.

The natural inquisitiveness common to children takes on special significance when we try to imagine that of Jesus as a little boy. From infancy, it seems, he was being led along a path of discovery to self-awareness about his divine nature while at the same time coming to appreciate the realities of his human existence. Jesus was gently brought into an increasing understanding of first his identity, then later the call on his life, and ultimately his true destiny and reason for coming to earth.

As the first glimmer of light heralds the dawn and then rises to its zenith, so Jesus' first inkling of who he was, and what he must do, may gradually have increased till the time of his baptism, when the full clarity of revelation was his. Perhaps it could be said that Jesus enjoyed spiritual insights incrementally; for example, while in prayer, or in meditating on God's word, or suddenly through a specific experience. As he grew, Jesus could view the Torah as a mirror, so to speak, seeing himself reflected and better enabling him to perceive more clearly who he was and what was required of him. He could look into "the perfect law that gives freedom, and continue in it, not forgetting what [he had] heard but doing it" *(James 1:25)*.

By taking our nature and becoming human, Jesus raised humanity – that's us! – to the level of the Son in relation to the Father. God has made *us* alive together with Christ and seated us with him in heavenly places *(Ephesians 2:4-7)*. As the Athanasian Creed says, "in Jesus Christ humanity has been assumed into God"[146]. A door has been opened for humankind to enter God's presence and be transformed and glorified. God, having united himself to humanity, invites us into unity with him, which is the destiny of all creation.

In Christ the last Adam, first of all, the goal is realised – the divine is joined to the human race. And through the Spirit, second, the divinisation of the world is beginning to be realised. In Christ, humanity is elevated to the life of God. What was intended in creation is accomplished by incarnation. By sharing flesh and blood, he has become the inauguration of a new humanity. Our healing has been accomplished by God's becoming human and restoring our brokenness from within his incarnate human life. All this is made efficacious by the Spirit because the power that raised Christ is now at work in us.

"Take hold of Jesus as a man and you will discover that he is God," wrote Martin Luther. Ironically, the church in its desire to affirm the

---

[146] Athanasian Creed para. 35

deity of Jesus has often been in danger of losing sight of his humanity, and then our image of him is distorted. "Christ's humanity," as theologian Richard Glover reminds us, "is the great hem of the garment, through which we touch his Godhead." This has been our goal: to explore how Jesus discovered his identity, calling, and mission, and from that foundation, to explore our own.

It is too easy to picture Jesus staid and solemn, distant and detached, and to reduce him to a long-faced, stained-glass image. This is precisely what we must not do, for Jesus was God in the flesh – all the bigness and power, goodness and glory, might and majesty of the universe, somehow incredibly wrapped up in the confines of humanity. Empowered by God's Spirit, we are called to reflect his humanity in our own, individually and corporately, as his body on earth.

At the Last Supper, Jesus made what must have seemed an outrageous claim to his disciples: that it was to their advantage that he would go away. In effect, he said they would be better off without him than with him.

> It is for your good that I am going away. Unless I go away, the Advocate will not come to you; but if I go, I will send him to you.
>
> *John 16:7*

Jesus knew he was limited to being in one place at one time. He knew too that, through the gift of the Spirit, the work he had accomplished over 1,000 days of ministry could be exponentially multiplied through his followers around the world, and down through the ages. As their humanity was empowered and filled by the Holy Spirit, they could continue his work as his body upon the earth.

In his ministry Jesus was surrounded by crowds of the irreligious, the spiritually confused, the undesirable, the unconvinced, and the morally bankrupt – ordinary people. People who, we might imagine, would be unlikely candidates for God to fulfil his purposes on earth. Yet Jesus has equipped the unqualified, the dubious, and the unfit for his service. He is able to use all who respond to him today.

> This is how love is made complete among us, so that we will have confidence on the day of judgment: In this world we are like Jesus.
>
> *1 John 4:17*

Believers, too, filled with the Holy Spirit *(Ephesians 5:18)*, can experience a *kenosis* – emptying of that which would hinder God's life-flow, by yielding independence to become dependent upon him, moment by moment, as Jesus did. He surrendered the independent use of his divine attributes in incarnation, notes Clark Pinnock, because self-emptying is characteristic of God. The Spirit enabled Jesus to live within the limits of human nature during his life.

The Son decided not to make use of divine attributes independently but experience what it would mean to be truly human. He depended on the Spirit for power to live his life and pursue his mission.

"The Son of God became man to enable men to become sons of God," observed C. S. Lewis. As Jesus gradually came to understand the implications of being God's Son, so Christians must grow in understanding of what it means to be God's children *(Romans 8:14-16)*. The process is a gradual unveiling of scripture to minds and spirits, a sensitising of spirits to a revelation of his Holy Spirit. Becoming a Christian is to be born again from above *(John 3:3)*, with a new nature *(2 Corinthians 5:17)*, not of something that will die like a seed, but something imperishable through the living and enduring word of God *(1 Peter 1:23)*.

For each individual it is the start of a discovery, a never-ending journey, where new insights and wonders are discerned and enjoyed. His life and work represent and correspond to the most important qualities of God himself – and he invites his people to join in. In the life of Jesus we see the beginning of a new creation. This is the pattern for humanity, the measure of what is truly human. Moreover, it is through Jesus that people come to understand the life of God. He is the revelation of God to man. Through Jesus it is recognised that God's nature is essentially relational, a fellowship of three, a communion of Persons, a community united by shared divinity. The uncreated, eternal, incomprehensible God is Trinity. Creation is a natural expression of God's life, and finite creatures find fulfilment in relation to him.

We cannot fully comprehend love apart from Jesus nor can we understand Jesus apart from love. As his life on earth drew to a close, Jesus recalled the Father's love for him: "You loved me before the creation of the world" *(John 17:24)*. Throughout his life on earth he continued to live in the consciousness of that love. He practised the presence of that love and from early childhood reflected it to others. To love God "with all your heart and with all your soul and with all your mind and with all your strength" *(Mark 12:30)* was at the heart of Jesus' own identity, teaching, and mission. It was his identity because God is love *(1 John 4:8)*, and he was the human face of God. To love God and neighbour was the essence of his teaching, and it is the essence of what God asks of each of his children (for example, *Mark 12:28-34; John 13:34)*. It was his mission: every aspect of his life and death perfectly demonstrated sacrificial love *(1 John 4:12)*.

Without an understanding of God's love, the identity, calling, and destiny of Jesus make no sense. God's love is the source and explanation behind it all. As sons and daughters of God, we too have a unique identity, calling, and destiny. While this may seem insignificant in comparison with that of Jesus, it is equally real. By revelation, written and spoken, we appreciate who we are in Christ, what our calling is, and our destiny. Such an understanding may take us years before it comes to fruition, as it did for Jesus, but it is something our Father longs for us to discover. The words and works of Jesus continue through us, his body on the earth, so that together – corporately – we may complete and fulfil the ultimate purpose for which humanity was created – to appreciate the grace, love, and fellowship of the three-in-one God, our maker and sustainer.

Hans Urs von Balthasar writes of Christ's service to others – in words applicable to both his hidden years and those spent in the public eye. But they also have relevance to all who seek to live as Christ-followers today.

> His service was a consequence of his self-awareness. Jesus did not fear people thinking him a servant. He had no false humility wanting people to think him better than he was, no concern that the others would rank him lower than them because of what he was doing; all of these concerns that prevent us from humbly serving another were completely absent in the actions of Jesus. He was completely aware of who he was, from whence he had come, and where he was going. So in full, confident self-awareness he was free to serve. Only people who are aware of who they really are, are free to humbly serve others. People who are insecure, who try to impress others, who hide feelings of inferiority, seek to sit in important places, be seen with the right people, and carefully avoid anything that would look like service, lack confident self-awareness. But they who know they are God's children,

who are followers of Jesus Christ, live in the security that they are right with God. So they can be willing to humbly serve.

Select Bibliography

Allen, C., *The Human Christ: The Search for the Historical Jesus* (Lion Publishing, Oxford, 1998)

Aristotle, *Politics* (CreateSpace Independent Publishing, 2015)

Aron, R., *A Boy Named Jesus: How the Early Years Shaped his Life* (Ulysses Press, Berkley, 1997)

Anselm, *Proslogion* (Penguin Classics, London, 1973)

Aplin, M., *Was Jesus Ever a Disciple of John the Baptist? A Historical Study* (Ph.D. Thesis, Edinburgh University, 2011)

Aslan, R., *Zealot: The Life and Times of Jesus of Nazareth* (Random House, New York, 2013)

Augustine, *The Trinity, in The Faith of the Early Fathers: St. Augustine to the End of the Patristic Age,* ed. W. A. Jurgens

Bailey, K. E., *Jacob and the Prodigal: How Jesus Retold Israel's Story* (InterVarsity, Downers Grove, 2003)

Balz, H. & Schneider, G. ed. *Exegetical Dictionary of the New Testament II* (Eerdmans, Grand Rapids, Michigan, 1991)

Barnett, P. W. *Jesus & the Rise of Early Christianity* (InterVarsity, Leicester, 2002)

Barnett, P. W., *Behind the Scenes of the New Testament* (InterVarsity, Leicester, 1990)

Bauckham, R., *Jude and the Relatives of Jesus in the Early Church* (T & T Clark, London, 1990)

Bauckham, R., *The Relatives of Jesus* (Themelios 21:2,1996)

Bayne, T., *The Inclusion Model of the Incarnation: Problems and Prospects,* Religious Studies, 37:2 (Cambridge University Press, Cambridge, June 2001)

Belcher, R. P. Jr., *The Messiah and the Psalms: Preaching Christ from All the Psalms* (Mentor, Christian Focus, Fearn, Scotland, 2006)

Bilezikian, G., *Community 101* (Zondervan, Grand Rapids, Michigan, 1997)

Borg, M. J. & Wright, N.T., *The Meaning of Jesus: Two Visions* (Harper, San Francisco, 1998)

Borland, J. A, *Christ in the Old Testament: Old Testament Appearances of Christ in Human Form* (Christian Focus, Fearn, Tain, Scotland, 2010)

Boyd, G., *God at War* (InterVarsity, Downers Grove, Michigan 1997)

Boyd, G., *Crucifixion of the Warrior God* (Fortress Press, Minneapolis, 2017)

Buechner, F., *Now and Then* (Harper, San Francisco; Reprint edition, 1991)

Calvin, J., *The Institutes of Religion* (Hendrickson, Peabody, Massachusetts, rev. ed., 2007)

Campbell, K., *What was Jesus' Occupation?* (Journal of the Evangelical Society, La Mirada, California, 48/3 Sept, 2005)

Carlston, C., in *Studying the Historical Jesus, Evaluations of the State of Current Research,* ed. Bruce Chilton & Chancey, M. A., *Greco-Roman Culture & the Galilee of Jesus* (Cambridge University Press, Cambridge, 2009)

Charlesworth J. H., *Notes from Jesus' Jewishness – Exploring the Place of Jesus in Early Judaism* (Crossroad Publishing, New York, 1991)

Chester, T., *The Message of Prayer* (InterVarsity, Leicester, 2003)

Crossan, J. D., *Jesus, a Revolutionary Biography* (Harper Collins, New York 1994)

David C. B., *Were there 204 Settlements in Galilee at the Time of Josephus Flavius?* (Journal of Jewish Studies, Oxford, 52.1., 2011)

Davis, S. T., Kendall D., & O'Collins, G. ed. *The Incarnation* (Oxford University Press, Oxford, 2002)

Dominian, J., *One Like Us: A Psychological Interpretation of Jesus* (Darton, Longman & Todd, London, 1998)

Donne, J., *Annunciation* and *Nativity* (Oxford University Press, Oxford, 2007)

Drummond, H., *The City without a Church* (Wilder, 2008)

Edersheim, A., *The Life and Times of Jesus the Messiah* (Hendrickson, Peabody, Massachusetts, 1883)

Erickson, M., *Who's Tampering with the Trinity? An Assessment of the Subordination Debate* (Kregel, Grand Rapids, 2009)

Graetz, H., *The History of the Jews from the Earliest Times to the Present Day* (Nabu Press, 2010)

Griffiin, J. H., *Black like me* (Souvenir Press, London, 50th ed., 2009)

Haber, S., *Going Up to Jerusalem: Purity, Pilgrimage and the Historical Jesus* in ed. Adele Reinhartz, *They Shall Purify Themselves. Essays on Purity in Early Judaism* (Society of Biblical Literature, Atlanta, 2008)

Hachlili, R., *Names and Nicknames of Jews in Second Temple Times, Eretz-Israel* 17, 1984)

Halls, C. L., *Jesus Reads the Psalms* (Xulon Press, Maitland, Florida, 2012)

Hill, E., (trans.), *The Works of Saint Augustine: A Translation for the 21st Century* (New City Press, New York, 1991)

Hodges, A., *Jesus – An Interview Across Time* (Kregel Publications, Grand Rapids, Michigan, 2nd ed., 2003)

Horsley, R.A., *Archaeology, History, and Society in Galilee: The Social Context of Jesus and the Rabbis* (Trinity International, Valley Forge, Pennsylvania, 1996)

Huggett, J., *Formed by the Desert, Heart to Heart Encounters with God* (Eagle, Washington, DC., 2000)

Irenaeus, *Against Heresies* (Ex Fontibus Co., 2015)

Jeremias, J., *The Prayers of Jesus* (Alec R. Allenson, Naperville, Illinois, 1967)

Josephus, F., *Jewish War* (Penguin Classics, London; rev. ed., 1981)

Josephus, F., *Jewish Antiquities* (Penguin Classics, London; rev. ed., 1981)

Juncker, G., *Christ As Angel: The Reclamation of a Primitive Title* (Trinity Journal 15:2 (Fall 1994)

Justin Martyr, *Dialogues* (Catholic University of America, Washington DC, 2003)

Kelly J. & Verny, T., *The Secret Life of the Unborn Child,* (Sphere Books, London, 1982)

Kempis, T. à, *The Imitation of Christ* (Penguin Classics, London, 2005)

Kimball, K., *Behold the Man: The Real Life of the Historical Jesus,* (Universal Publishers, Irvine, California, 2002)

Kittel, *Theological Dictionary of the New Testament* (Eerdmans, Grand Rapids, Michigan, 1985)

Kropf, R. W., *The Faith of Jesus – the Jesus of History and the Stages of Faith* (Wipf & Stock, Eugene, Oregon, 2006)

Leo, *The Tome of Leo (www.ccel.org/ccel/schaff/npnf214.xi.vii.html)*

Lewis, C. S., *Mere Christianity* (Geoffrey Bles, London, 1952)

Longman, T. III, & Dillard R., *Introduction to the Old Testament* (Zondervan, Grand Rapids, Michigan, 2006)

Lucado, M., *God Came Near: God's Perfect Gift* (Thomas Nelson, Nashville, Tennessee; Reprint Ed., 2013)

Luther, M., *First Lectures on the Psalms, Psalms 1-75, Luther's Works* (ed. Hilton C. Oswald; 56 vols., Concordia, Missouri, 1974)

Luther, M., *We Praise, O Christ, Your Holy Name* (ed. Hilton C. Oswald; 56 vols., Concordia, Missouri, 1974)

Luther, M., *Word and Sacrament in Luther's Works* (ed. Hilton C. Oswald; 56 vols., Concordia, Missouri, 1974)

MacDonald, G., *That Holy Thing* (Arthur Quiller-Couch, ed., *The Oxford Book of English Verse: 1250-1900,* Oxford, 1919)

McKnight, S., *Praying with the Church* (Paraclete Press, Brewster, Massachusetts, 2006)

Metcalfe, J., *The Birth of Jesus Christ* (John Metcalfe Publishing, Tylers Green, Buckinghamshire, 1993)

Morris, T., *Our Idea of God: An Introduction to Philosophical Theology* (Regent College, Vancouver, 2002)

Motyer, A., *The Prophecy of Isaiah* (InterVarsity Press, Leicester ,1993)

Murray, A., *Humility – The Beauty of Holiness* (CreateSpace, Scotts Valley, California, 2014)

Oord, T. J., *The Uncontrolling Love of God – An Open and Relational Account of Providence* (InterVarsity, Downers Grove, Illinois, 2015)

Oursler, F., *The Greatest Story Ever Told* (Penguin Random House, London, 1989)

Oxenford, J., *The Hidden Years* (Longmans, Green & Co., New York & London, Reprinted, 1952)

Page, N., *What Happened to the Ark of the Covenant and Other Bible Mysteries* (Authentic Media, Milton Keynes, 2007)

Pilch, J. C., *The Cultural World of Jesus* (Liturgical Press, Minnesota, 1996)

Pinero, A., *The Hidden Life of Jesus* (Cascade Books, Wipf & Stock, Eugene, Oregon, 2016)

Pinnock, C., *Flame of Love, A Theology of the Holy Spirit* (InterVarsity Press, Leicester, 1996)

Ponsonby, S., *God inside out – An In-depth Study of the Holy Spirit* (Pearl Books, Edinburgh, 2015)

Nelson-Pallmeyer J., *Jesus against Christianity: reclaiming the missing Jesus* (Trinity International, Bloomsbury, London)

Reed, J. L., *Archaeology & The Galilean Jesus: A Re-examination of the Evidence* (Trinity, Harrisburg, Pennsylvania, 2000)

Rice, A., *Christ the Lord, the Road to Cana* (Arrow Books, Random House, London, 2009)

Rice, A., *Christ the Lord: Out of Egypt* (Arrow Books, Random House, London, 2005)

St John of the Cross, *The Spiritual Canticle in Collected Works of St. John of the Cross* (ICS Publications, Washington DC, 1991)

St John of the Cross, *The Ascent of Mount Carmel in Collected Works of St. John of the Cross* (ICS Publications, Washington DC, 1991)

Sanders, E. P., *Jesus in Historical Context* (Theology Today, 50.3, 1993)

Sanders, J., *The God Who Risks: A Theology of Providence* (InterVarsity, Downers Grove, Illinois, 1998)

Sauer, E., *Triumph of the Crucified* (Eerdmans, Michigan, 1985)

Sawyer, J. F. A., *The Fifth Gospel, Isaiah in the History of Christianity* (Cambridge University Press, Cambridge, 1996)

Schleiermacher, F., *Speeches on Religion,* Speech 2, 1799, Westminster (Knox Press, Louisville, Kentucky, 1994)

Sire, J., *Praying the Prayers of Jesus* (InterVarsity, Leicester, 2007)

Sister Margaret Magdalen, *Jesus Man of Prayer* (Hodder & Stoughton, London, 2nd ed., 1991)

Stern, D., *Jewish New Testament Commentary* (Jewish NT publications, Maryland, 1992)

Storms S., *The Most Amazing Verse in the Bible,* February 20, 2010, quoted in Andreas J. Kostenberger & Stewart, A. E., *The First Days of Jesus* (Crossway, Illinois, 2015)

Stott, J. R. W., *The Message of Romans, The Bible Speaks Today* (InterVarsity, Leicester, 1994)

Swidler, L., *Jesus was a Feminist* (Sheed & Ward, Kansas City, 2007)

Tadg Gaelach O Suilleabhaim, *Pious Miscellany*

Taylor, J.E., *What did Jesus look like?* (Bloomsbury, London, 2018)

Thiessen, K. H., *Jesus and Women in the Gospel of John* (Direction Journal 19.2, 1990)

Travis, S., *The Galilee Jesus Knew* (Grove, B62, 2011, Ridley Hall, Cambridge)

Turner S., *Up to Date* (Hodder & Stoughton, London, 1983)

Vermes, G., *Jesus and the World of Judaism* (Fortress, Minneapolis, Minnesota, 1983)

Vermes, G. *The Changing Faces of Jesus* (Penguin, London, 2000)

Von Balthasar, H. U., *Explorations in Theology: The Word made Flesh* (Ignatius Press, San Francisco, 1993)

Von Balthasar, H. U., *Prayer* (Ignatius Press, San Francisco, 1986)

Wallace, D., *When Did Jesus Know? The Translation of Aorist and Perfect Participles for Verbs of Perception in the Gospels* (bible.org, 2004)

Walvoord, J. F., *Jesus Christ our Lord* (Moody Press, Chicago, 1969)

Ward, K., God, *A Guide for the Perplexed* (One World, London, 2002)

Warfield, B.B., *Emotional Life of Our Lord* (P&R, Phillipsburg, New Jersey, 1950)

Warfield, B. B., *The Person and Work of Christ* (P&R, Phillipsburg, New Jersey, 1950)

Wenham, J., *Christ and the Bible* (Wipf & Stock, Eugene, Oregon, 3rd ed., 2009)

Wilson, A.N., *Jesus* (Pimlico, London, 2003)

Witherington III, B., *The Jesus Quest; The Third Search for the Jew of Nazareth* (Paternoster, Carlisle, 1995)

Weatherhead, I. D., *A Plain Man looks at the Cross* (Independent Press, 1948)

Wright, N.T., *Jesus and the Victory of God: Christian Origins and the Question of God* (Fortress, Minneapolis, Minnesota, 1996)

Wright, N.T., *The Challenge of Jesus, Rediscovering who Jesus was and is* (InterVarsity, Leicester, 2015)

Yancey, P., *The Bible Jesus Read* (Zondervan, Grand Rapids, Michigan, 1999)

Yancey, P., *The Jesus I Never Knew* (Zondervan, Grand Rapids, Michigan, 1995)

Printed in Great Britain
by Amazon

14617367R00113